THIS BOOK

which appears at the time of the Empire
Exhibition in Glasgow was edited by
a Scotsman who, along with all the
contributors, lives and works in Scotland.
It has been printed and bound and is
published by Oliver and Boyd, who have
conducted their business in Edinburgh
since the year 1778. The paper on which
it was printed was made by Henry Bruce
& Sons Ltd. of Currie, Midlothian, and
the blocks for the illustrations were made
by Hislop & Day Ltd. of Edinburgh.

Scottish Country : A Miniature of the Rural Scene

SCOTLAND—1938

TWENTY-FIVE IMPRESSIONS

EDITED BY

J. R. ALLAN

Author of *Down on the Farm* and *Farmer's Boy*

OLIVER AND BOYD

EDINBURGH: TWEEDDALE COURT

LONDON: 98 GREAT RUSSELL STREET, W.C.

PRINTED IN GREAT BRITAIN BY
OLIVER AND BOYD LTD., EDINBURGH

CONTENTS

v

ILLUSTRATIONS

INTRODUCING THE COMPANY

THIS book is intended for three classes of reader —for those who come from abroad to see Scotland, for those who would like to come but cannot spare the time, and for all others who are good enough to buy or borrow it.

The plan of the book is very simple. We hope to give you a series of impressions, which, taken together, will be a picture of Scotland as it is to-day. We have deliberately chosen this method as the best in the circumstances; for we wished to have a variety of minds on the job and we knew that if we set a number of people writing to a rigid plan we were bound to get a certain amount of routine matter written in a dull way. So we made a plan that would allow as much freedom as possible. We found people that have lively minds and we said to each of them, " We know you are interested in such-and-such ; write us a piece about that aspect of it which interests you most." Each has written his piece in the way that he wished to write it, and so we hope that the book has one of the best sorts of unity—immediate interest in the subject of discussion, whatever it may be.

We have omitted the misery and degradation of which Scotland has a full share, because these are common to all countries in this day and age, and we wished to concentrate on things that seemed essentially Scottish.

Let us now introduce the company and their subjects.

The first section contains four pieces on Scottish country. It was, we thought, impossible to put the whole Scottish countryside into ten thousand words, so we got a man from the north and one from the south and one from the east and invited them to write on anything that would express the spirit of their region. So Eric Linklater, the author of *Juan in America* and *Ripeness is All*, has written about the Orkney farmers who have made so much of such indifferent land. Considering that that has been the history of Scotland in so many other things, we are pleased that this piece should open the serious business of the book.

Then Robin Jay, of the *Scottish Field*, has taken a bang at the Border. He has been a Rugby football player in his time, so he approaches the Border with the appropriate spirit of a forward going into a loose maul, ready to give knocks and still have a friendly drink at the little pub round the corner after the game.

George Harvey, we feel, had a very difficult job in trying to express that intangible and devastating quality called " East Coast," which is found at its perfection in the Buchan shoulder of Aberdeenshire. But he knows his subject—perhaps no one knows it better—for he belongs to Aberdeen, works as a journalist there, is a master of all the local dialects from Gallowgate to Queen's Road, and yet can see Aberdeen with the detachment of one sitting on top of the Mitchell Tower.

The West was rather a problem, because it has so many problems of its own that they would have required a whole book to themselves. Besides there has been a very great deal written about the Highlands in the last twenty years, either on its economic troubles or in extravagant praise of its romantic beauty. We did not wish to add any more to either heap. Therefore we asked Alastair Borthwick to write about walking and climbing in Scotland, with particular reference to the Highlands. As you might expect from one who speaks in such a light fashion about thirty miles a day, this writer is a young man, but he has a knowledge of walking and climbing in the lonelier parts of Scotland that would have prematurely aged a less resilient spirit.

The second part of the book deals with the cities and the people that live in them. It is fitting that James Bridie's examination of urban manners should be the first piece in this section, for his plays, such as *The Anatomist, The Black Eye* and *Storm in a Teacup* have shown him as a diverting critic of current society. James Bridie is also Dr O. H. Mavor, which may give him an anatomical approach to our follies : here some of the more amusing ones are dissected.

There are of course several cities in Scotland, but only Edinburgh and Glasgow have got chapters to themselves. We hope that Dundee and Aberdeen (and Brechin and Elgin) will forgive the omissions, caused not through lack of appreciation but only through lack of room. Besides, we think that A. D. Mackie has caught very well the outer restraint and inner warmth that are common to the people of all the East Coast cities. Though Mr Mackie is an Edinburgh man he can look at his native town and at Scotland with a blessed detachment given by several years in the West Indies before he returned home, but not nearer home than Glasgow.

The chapter on Glasgow contains its own apology and nothing need be said about it here.

The third part—on work—is rather different from the rest of the book, for we have tried to make it a short comprehensive survey. C. A. Oakley and Ian Macpherson have many claims to be considered experts here, for Mr Oakley as an industrial psychologist has an extensive knowledge of the diversity of Scottish trades, and Mr Macpherson was concerned lately with a service for helping rural tradesmen to adapt themselves to changing conditions. These two gentlemen have one thing in common, that they have both been on the teaching staff of Aberdeen University. Otherwise they are quite dissimilar, for Mr Oakley is chairman of the Glasgow Junior Chamber of Commerce and writes about vocational guidance, while Mr Macpherson is now a sheep farmer in the north and has written some fine novels, including *Pride in the Valley*, *Shepherd's Calendar* and *Land of our Fathers*.

The writer of the piece about agriculture, overcome in the presence of such experts, wishes to make a personal explanation. It had been arranged that Mr Joseph Duncan, the distinguished agricultural economist, should write the article but Mr Duncan was taken ill and the present writer had to do the job instead. It is therefore written from an observer's point of view and shows less mild forbearance and sympathetic understanding towards the farmers than they would have expected from Mr Duncan.

In all this part we have tried to show how industries are adapting themselves to modern conditions. We are not ignorant that some industries are finding it difficult to do so, and that there are factors, such as the over-centralising influence of London, which intensify our problems. Anyone who comes to Scotland will soon find out these things for himself.

The fourth part concerns the houses where the people live and the buildings where they work.

Scotland has not great resources of old building, such as may be found in parts of England, but there are some fine examples of the ancient native style. George Scott-Moncrieff tells you where you may find some of them. He cares for houses not because they are old but only because they are beautiful, and he analyses that beauty in a fitly architected style. He is neither old nor an antiquary, but young, and author among other things of a novel about Soho, called *Café Bar*, that made a considerable reputation.

Robert Hurd also is young and full of enthusiasm, a quality deplorably lacking in Scotland just now. He is an architect who would like to see Scotland saved from Victorian whimsies and modern bungalows through the re-creation of a good native style of building. If his enthusiasm can survive the drag of conservatism, indifference and simple bad taste, he may leave Scotland less comically housed than he found her.

Then there is Education, so essential to any progress. Since our education system is famous, we asked Dr Peddie, secretary of the National Committee for the Training of Teachers, to describe that system. He has held closely to his brief like a good advocate, and has refrained from saying any of the things that, as an administrator, he must feel about those who would hinder the working of any system however good. And here, we thought, was a chance for an old Scottish quality that still survives to-day. There is still a spirit of criticism in Scotland that makes people examine even our most sacred institutions without respect or mercy. That spirit has not quickened the whole nation : indeed we may suspect that the " Here's tae us, wha's like us " attitude is growing stronger ; but there are a few who doubt if every Scottish institution is the very best in the best of all possible worlds and they do not spare themselves in saying so. The person who has written the companion to Dr Peddie's article is one of them. His (or her) anonymity is preserved for the sole reason that he (or she) is speaking not for himself (or herself) alone but for many others. So identity remains a secret, but we can say this much—he (or she) is not Dr Peddie. Nor is the article an attack on, or a reply to, Dr Peddie's account of the system.

The Arts. Here we have done no more than offer you an introduction to what civilised entertainment can be found inside our borders. William Power, who shows the way through the generations of our books, is the father of our company, but he retains the divine quality of enthusiasm, and after a lifetime spent among books he can still see them as something more enduring than stone and lime. " Hal o' the Wynd " is another journalist, a young one this time, and his article may be regarded as the notes of a man to whom the arts are professional incidents in a busy working life, so you might read the notes as if they were table-talk by a knowledgeable man over lunch in the city. Colm Brogan's discourse on the Glasgow comedians might be good conversation heard in the quiet corner of a Glasgow public house ; Mr Brogan has such a grand appreciation of the essential Glasgow so richly set on the stage by Tommy Lorne and Tommy Morgan. Then, since good eating and wise drinking are essential to entertainment and the arts, Will Y. Darling tells you about some of the dishes and the drinks that are indigenous to Scotland and do us credit.

Out of the many games, we have chosen Association Football, Rugby Football and Golf because the passions they rouse in their various publics most readily show forth the Scottish nature. The versatile Mr Brogan has written about Association Football in as lively manner as about the Glasgow comedians, and we are not surprised at that for there is a community of spirit between the two subjects. R. N. Biles, who combines a taste for sport with an appreciation of the finer arts, recalls some of the notable Rugby players of recent years with a grace in writing something like the physical grace with which G. P. S. Macpherson used to enchant the Murrayfield crowds. And Sam McKinlay, a golfer who has had a very fine record in international matches, sums up the achievements of the young Scottish amateurs who are now coming into their best years.

Our book ends with a number of pieces that may be called diversions. We had thought that we might offer you a short story or two but there do not seem to be many distinguished short stories written by Scotsmen just now. However, there is one thing that Scots writers do very well and that is to sketch a character, so we have collected three characters and a conversation piece for your entertainment.

First, Mr James Fergusson's sketch of his ancestor, Sir Adam Fergusson of Kilkerran in Ayrshire, charming in its execution and interesting for its subject, who was one of the men that redeemed rural Scotland from the wilderness. Second, the sketch of Dainty Daniel, a north-east character, by George Burnett, himself a native of Aberdeenshire. Mr Fergusson and Mr Burnett are both on the executive staff of the B.B.C. in Scotland. The third character sketch concerns the imaginative David, a child that must have escaped the evils of the education system alleged in the article already mentioned. John S. Buist who wrote it is another of the Glasgow journalists although a native of the East Coast. He also wrote, under the name of Adam Kennedy, a brave experiment in Braid Scots, called *Orra Boughs*. " Sweet Saturday Night," which ends the book, sets a nice note on which to say good-bye ; and if you want to find a social significance in it, you may care to think upon the fact that the Scottish Saturday Night comes immediately before the Scottish Sabbath.

These, then, are our company and this is our book.

We must not stand between you and the business any longer. But we would just sum the matter quite shortly. This book has not any particular point of view for each of our company has his own opinions and Scotsmen do not readily agree. The writers, with two or three exceptions, are on the younger side of forty and all live and work in Scotland. There perhaps you *may* find a common point of view, for all of them are people of some imagination and intelligence and they would like the country they live in to be an agreeable, civilised one. So we think you will find in this book either a lively appreciation of the good things we have, or a strong intention to change those that are bad. At least we hope there is none of that weary thing—a limp regret for past glories ; or of that still wearier thing—an acceptance of good and bad alike because nothing matters much. The Scots are a nation to whom different things at different times have mattered greatly. It would be well that it were always so.

And now we wish you refreshment in all that comes hereafter.

BLAIRLOGIE IN STIRLINGSHIRE.
April 1938.

NORTH, SOUTH, EAST, WEST
THE CHARMS OF SCOTTISH COUNTRY

A

by
ERIC LINKLATER

The Orkney Islands are Scotland's Grand Surprise, for in the very place where you might expect the ultimate desolation, you find one of the best farmed parts of the country

THE ORKNEY FARMERS

A FEW miles west of Kirkwall there is a ridge of hill called at the one end Lyradale, at the other the Keelylang. It gives a good view, to the south, of the great basin of Scapa Flow, the dark walls of Hoy, and the yellowish hills of Caithness ; and to the north it looks over the shallow Bay of Firth to a chequered landscape of square fields, of moorland smoothly rising, and islets floating on a calm horizon. There are half-a-hundred islands in the archipelago— not counting Heather-Blether, which comes and goes —and some have so long a history that the relics of their earliest inhabitants are as cold as any thought of Nineveh and Tyre ; and others could tell only an innocent tale of seals about the shore and a few stormy petrels in deserted rabbit-burrows. Some that were once important have lost their fame, and others that were disregarded are now put to good use ; for history has a way of shifting its emphasis.

Almost below the observer on the ridge of hill, as he faces northward, are two islets, round and flat as tea-plates, that epitomise a thousand years of change. On Damsay, the outer one, are the pointed gables of a ruined house ; on the Holm of Grimbister a snug farm and well-kept fields. Damsay was once a goal of pilgrimage ; it sheltered that great man, Sweyn

Asleifson, last of the Vikings, on the night he spoiled the Yule feast of Earl Paul by killing the Earl's champion, Sweyn Breastrope ; and another Yule it saw the murder of Earl Erlend, an agreeable youth, but drunk at the time. In the heroic age of Orkney, Damsay was an island of significance—and now it grazes a few native sheep, and may give a morning's good duck-shooting.

But the Holm of Grimbister has come up in the world. The Sagas make no mention of it ; but nowadays, in the month of August especially, it is much in the news because the farmer breeds cattle that, for the past few years, have taken the highest award at the County Show. Last year a judge—no Orkneyman, full of native prejudice, but a man from Aberdeenshire, Perthshire, somewhere in the south—said there was not a better crossbred cow in Scotland than the prize-winning beast from the Holm of Grimbister. That is the sort of thing that nowadays we feed our pride upon ; and when the circumstances are considered, it may be thought that this peaceful triumph is more significant than Sweyn's timely killing of Sweyn Breastrope, or the murder of young Erlend.

The Holm of Grimbister is about forty acres in extent, and the stock consists of approximately six cows, six young cattle, six calves ; a pair of horses, or perhaps three ; and two or three sheep. Now whether the be-medalled cow is, or is not, the best animal of its kind in Scotland does not really matter ; but it is certainly a cow of championship class, and for two reasons that does matter. In the first place it shows what can be done on a farm that in many parts of the country would be considered little better than a croft, and so would be farmed after the crofting fashion ; and secondly, it indicates a standard of farming that is by no means uncommon in Orkney. In January of this year fifty yearling bulls, locally bred, were locally sold at an average price of thirty-nine guineas, the top price being seventy-eight guineas. Nearly all these bulls came from small farms and went to other small farms. Nor is the dam neglected so that an extravagant price may be given for the sire. There is, indeed, an almost Virgilian regard for the cow—Virgil's advice to the farmer was *corpora præcipue matrum legat*—and it is a common thing to see in a modest little field a small herd of beautifully bred level beasts.

The average farm is from twenty-five to forty acres of arable land, with some hill ground that rarely gives anything but peat. Twenty-five acres will support a family without ancillary employment ; seventy acres should give a man the means to own a motor-car. The farmer is typically the owner of his land. His cattle for the most part are pure-bred Aberdeen-Angus ; his horses are Clydesdales properly begotten by recognised sires ; and his sheep, if he has outrun for them, are Cheviots. If he merely keeps three or four, they will be of a native-bred Leicester type. Poultry are reared and kept in large numbers. The stock is of good quality because the farmer has learnt that good quality pays, and because—but I am not sure whether this is not the elder reason—because of the intensity of his pride in it. The local cattle shows are the chief events of the year, there are huge entry-lists, and the competition is eager.

Now the Orkney farmer has many difficulties to contend with. Much of his land is not naturally rich. It must be well drained, well tended, heavily fed with manures. Our climate could be better ; summer is late in coming, and sometimes loth to stay. And the farmer is cut off from his southern market by a hundred and thirty miles of sea and linked to it only by the monopoly of a steamship company whose freights are dear : it costs twenty-five shillings to ship a fat beast to Aberdeen, half-a-crown or three shillings to carry a sheep. But in spite of these handicaps the farmer is relatively prosperous, and within his limits successful. Orkney, indeed, has now a modest name for well-being, and after many centuries we are again beginning to be cried-up in the world a little.

And why ? It may be that the Orkneyman has discovered an economic size of farm ; or the pride of ownership may urge him to use his wits as well as his strength ; and perhaps Sweyn Asleifson and the Earls of whom the Saga tells have something to do with it. I think they have. Norse blood and Norse character-istics are still dominant in the islands. I know fairly well the sagas of Iceland and Norway, and the style of speech in them ; and for a good many years I have been familiar with the speech of my Orkney neighbours of to-day ; and sometimes they are like as two peas. There is the same humour, a humour of understatement, of the objective eye and the balancing intelligence. There is a great appreciation of irony. There is— though it may seem extravagant to say so—there is something of the same æsthetic judgment of conduct. Much is forgiven, as it was in saga times, to anyone who behaves in character.

This æsthetic appreciation is also shown by the style of our gossiping, which is rarely truthful, but must be congruous. It should be ingenious, but it must fit the person of whom it is told—and so it is judged. It is singularly devoid of malice. It may be, and often is, scandalous ; but I have listened to a great deal of it, and invented some, and I have always been aware that its main appeal lay not in the slighting of any-one's character, but in the way it fitted that character. We prize the art of gossip rather than its content.

Of the similarity between contemporary speech and the classic address of the Norsemen, here is a slight example : A farmer, whom I know well, had gone to Thurso to the ram sales. He bought three, for two of which he paid an ordinary £7 or £8 ; but the third he bought at the extravagant and most unusual price of £16. One of the three was for a neighbour, who was to have his pick of them at the price paid. The farmer brought them home, and his son was filled with admiration for the expensive one, which was quite obviously the best. And which of the other two, he asked, was their neighbour to get ?

His father said he had promised to give him the pick of the three. His son protested, saying they must certainly keep the best one for themselves, but in vain. His father would stand by his word, and no argument could move him. Then the son asked what his father had paid for the rams, and after a little delay—after enquiring " What would thoo say ? " and so forth—he answered : " Seven pounds and eight pounds for that and that, and sixteen for the other."

Slowly a smile appeared on the face of his son. " Weel may thoo gie Ronald his choice," he said.

Well, there is the very trick and tone of the sagas. There is the comprehension of a whole situation, with insight into the beginning of it, understanding of the end of it, and an almost epigrammatic expression of it. It is the voice of Gunnar speaking, or Skarphedinn.

The paradox of an eager and persistent interest in

money, combined with large generosity, is also common to Orkney and the saga people. A small farmer must, of course, be interested in money, and worry a bargain to its last shilling if he is going to live at all ; but having spent the afternoon haggling over the price of an ox, and finally getting his ultimate five shillings with half-a-crown back for a luckpenny, he need not be anciently open-handed to the first passer-by. But hospitality is still a habit rather than a conscious virtue here, and there is much giving of small presents. The Norsemen, too, were bitter-hard bargainers, and then would spend all their profit on the entertaining of their friends. But the Norsemen carried their bargaining to bed with them, and made a business arrangement of marriage ; and here there seems to be no notion whatever of marrying to advantage. I have never heard of a case where either bride or groom had been thought to have considered the material benefit of an alliance, and this shows a curious difference from the sentiment of Aberdeenshire, for example, where such a motive is common enough to have created a proverbial expression that describes the process.

But these virtues are not unaccompanied by northern disabilities. There is perhaps an excessive individualism in Orkney. A man will rely on himself, stubbornly and with jealous regard for his self-reliance, though to combine with his neighbours would give him many advantages. Co-operation would certainly be a great help in the problem of marketing, and by the acceptance of certain general standards the value of minor produce could easily be increased. But they never will co-operate. The Jews and the Arabs will sit in unity together before the neighbouring minute villages of Harray and Dounby, and the Nazi will lie down with the Communist long before Kirkwall and Stromness are reconciled.—And perhaps they are right. One can pay too high a price for another pound of profit, and life would be less interesting without local enmities.

The most serious deficiency of life in the islands is the lack of any indigenous culture. There is no native literature, save the Saga, no native music, or style of dancing. A few riddles, charms, and rhymes survived till a generation or two ago, but even they are forgotten now. This unfortunate poverty is almost certainly due to the fact that after the islands had been pledged to Scotland they were, for centuries, so tyrannously misruled that life was reduced to a mere subsistence level. The Norse landowners, small though they were, were deliberately spoiled of their heritage, and with it they must have lost, first the opportunity, and then the aptitude for story-telling and poetry-making which continued to mark and bless their cousins in Iceland. We have, then, no literature. We are also a voiceless, tuneless people, and though dancing is exceedingly popular, it is very badly performed. At country dances they execute reels and other Scotch dances with some vigour, but carelessly and without grace ; and with obvious liking they tread the dreary measure of some trumpery piece of shuffling that is vaguely reminiscent of yesterday's fashion in the South.

But, as I have said, there is an excuse for this poverty. In the innermost parts and the outer isles of Orkney, the English language is hardly more than two hundred years old, and that is no time to make a literature. Two hundred years ago we were still struggling with famine conditions, the heritage of the Scotch earls. It is only within the last half-century that the people—apart from a few small lairds and a leash of merchants in Kirkwall—have had the smallest surplus of time, money, or strength to spend on the graces of life. Not since the Norsemen were spoiled of their land have they had any opportunity to create or nurse a culture. We are beginning to have that opportunity now—but whether we shall recognise it for what it is worth, I do not know. There are little signs here and there. There is plenty of intelligence, and with their emotional insularity the people combine much interest in the outside world, and very often a shrewd appreciation of its events and personalities. But there is no near tradition of any art on which to build, nor any urgent desire, as yet, to express or interpret or create addition to the new ways of life. They are still too new, perhaps. They have not been digested yet.

That is the difficulty, I think. One may say that Damsay is too far away from us, and the Holm of Grimbister too near. But both are parts of the same Orkney, and if you stand on the ridge between Lyradale and the Keelylang, with a kestrel in the air and a hen-harrier farther down the hill—patterns of patience and far-sightedness—you may see a shadow on the horizon that you will not find on the map. Heather-Blether, perhaps, the island that has no substance. But perhaps—though I shall not quote the odds—perhaps an island compact of the near and the far, the old and new, whose soil should be richer than either.

by
ROBIN JAY

The Border breeds enthusiasm, so you
will find no reservations, no half-
heartedness, in this piece about the
lively inhabitants of the frontier

THE BORDER

AND now let us take a bang at the Border, because
the hardy Borderers themselves are all for
taking a bang at any given subject. In their
dealings with each other, and with the world outbye,
they prefer the direct assault, the straight approach.
It is not their habit to beat about the bush, or to butter
parsnips with soft words. So we can dispense with
preamble and get to the point at once. And the point
about the Border is simply that it is still a frontier
territory, inhabited by a vigorous, forthright, con-
versative, jolly, and occasionally bellicose people.
Nearly all of the country between Berwick and the
Solway was once a battleground, and not very long
ago at that.

There are, I suppose, corners of Scotland in which the
simple traveller who is really looking for excitement
can be more swiftly accommodated. The Bridgeton
district of Glasgow, for example, has a pretty sensational
record for criminal assault and indiscriminate mayhem.
The Coolins and the Cairngorms are high and famous
hills ; and if you hanker after perilous pleasure on the
deep, there's a lot to be said for a trip through the
Pentland Firth in a sailing dinghy. But sticking
exclusively to facilities for hunting, shooting, and
fishing (and hiking, biking, hill-walking, rugby football,

11

the gracious country life, salmon-poaching, versifying, love-making, pub-crawls, vigorous debate, or even a bout of fisticuffs), all to be conducted in a spirit of good clean fun, commend me to the Border. For here is a mountainy and primitive country with room enough for virile men to bang about at will—agreeably as the natives do, or belligerently as the English did in the olden time, filling the air with dust and oaths. There are times even now when the Border dust still flies in that way.

Not that the casual tourist is ever likely to notice, bless his timid heart. Heavens, no ! The Border tourist route is beautifully organised, as these things often are. The sign-posting has been done meticulously. In the season the motor coaches whizz round the chosen spots like hobbyhorses at a fair—Abbotsford and the four Abbeys (Melrose, Dryburgh, Kelso and Jedburgh), St Mary's Loch and Yarrow, Moffat and the Beef Tub, Gretna and Dumfries. And the chosen spots are enough, perhaps, to be going on with. They are all pretty, romantical, domesticated or easily definable. If you are acquainted with the novels and poems of Sir Walter Scott, you know as much as need be known about their past ; their present is, more or less, an open book—a plain tale of farming, and marketing, and manufacturing, and shopkeeping, and State housing schemes, and civic ambition, and neigh-bourly affection, and back-answers, and the eternal war between private enterprise and the collective conscience.

But there is more to the Border than that. There is a wilder history that goes back without a break to the time of Wallace, and beyond that in legend. Else-where in Scotland you have to dig for history under the debris of the Industrial Revolution. Along the Border

12

history stares at you from every howe and hillock, from almost every street corner : Jedburgh has a house in which Mary Queen of Scots once lay sick of a fever and nearly died. In Berwick, there is still the Castle in which Edward I imprisoned the Countess of Buchan for having dared to crown the Bruce, King of Scotland. Carlisle Castle is the very stronghold from which the Scots rescued Kinmont Willie ; and along the valleys there are the little peel towers that suffered in this raid or that notorious foray—four, five, ay even six centuries ago. These things have left their mark inevitably in the bluff, rumbustious character of the people. They explain, in part at least, the truculent pride with which the Teries of Hawick proclaim (in song) that " Hawick's Queen o' a' the Border," and the persistence of the Souters of Selkirk in damning (also in song) their benevolent and invariably charming neighbour, the Earl of Home. And they have no parallel in the other provinces of Scotland or England.

Indeed, in its overweening sense of history and in its traditional hatreds, the Border almost resembles Ireland. Also, the most violent of its hatreds all have their roots in the old wars with the English. The fact that for hundreds of years it was rammed hard against a ruthless and superior enemy hardened the Border character, you might say, and isolation has done the rest. So, bless my Sam, this affinity with Ireland is no fanciful invention ; it sticks out a mile. But there is this distinction to be noted : the traditional hatreds of Ireland are still liable to find expression in a rattle of pistol shots or a bit of bomb-throwing, whereas the Border hates have all been idealised, and seldom lead to violence, except on the football field. For the Borderers can laugh and laugh and laugh at their own idiosyncrasies. Quite frequently they do, too, but it is unwise to join too heartily in the laughter : they might misunderstand. And, as in Ireland, they never laugh at their ancestry. Nor at the antique ballads. Nor at the native dialect, in which all sorts of extra-ordinary things happen to vowels. Again, they hate to be reminded that the Border is largely a backward and relatively poor province. It is safer to praise the Border rivers, with their magical-mystery names— Tweed, Whitadder, Teviot, Jed, Leader, Gala, Ettrick, Yarrow, Liddel, Annan, Esk, Lyne and Nith. And how they merit praise !

Looking up Tweedside from Berwick, or Coldstream, or even Kelso you might be forgiven for believing that the Border is just another slice of farmer's glory. To the North of these delectable burghs there is always the Merse, the most compact and level plain in Scotland. Actually it extends to a hundred and thirty thousand acres, most of them arable. It produces huge crops of barley of superlative quality, and ponderable quantities of potatoes, and on that deep generous soil the farmers, ancient and modern, stick as closely as possible to the old four-course rotation and a comfortable faith in Providence. But the Merse, big as it is, is contained entirely in Berwick and Roxburgh, and these are only two of the Border's Scottish counties. There are three others that are less fortunately situated. Four-fifths of the area of Selkirkshire, for example, and three-quarters of Peebles, consist of rough upland pasture. Dumfries has its share of rough ground, too. And these areas, for the reason that nothing else could find a living on them, are given over to sheep—thousands and thousands of hardy Cheviots, with here and there a flock of Blackfaces looking as though they had just come in from the Highlands and liked the change enormously. Naturally, too, for the Border hills are grass-grown to their summits. (There is moderate grazing even on Broad Law, which at 2723 feet is the highest hill in the South of Scotland.) And the Border shepherds are justly acknowledged to be the wisest in the world— great lean fellows with upturned toes to their boots, and a positive passion for solitude. In youth and middle life they go over their native hills with the ease and action of Paavo Nurmi, the Flying Finn, and in age they put on the dignity of the Prophets. Unless you learned it from them, you could walk the Border from one end to the other, and never be informed that practically all the little hills, up to 800 feet anyhow, are Old Red Sandstone, while the high tops are just so many outcrops of the older Silurian rocks.

But we did not begin to-day to consider the Border geologically, or bathy-orographically, or agriculturally or even historically, although the history is important. The simple visitor who concentrated on these things and got caught up in a Common Riding would look pretty foolish, and sooner or later every simple visitor to the Middle Border has that shattering experience. There are five of them—Hawick, Selkirk, Peebles, Langholm and Lauder—and they occur in June and July. Also, there is at Galashiels about the same time a Gathering that is as near as ninepence a Common Riding without a common. They differ slightly in form, but everywhere the accompaniments are the same—spectacle and dancing and song. Carnival, in short. It is the Border's own particular brand of midsummer madness. And it will stand a little explication.

Well, you must have gathered that so recently as

15

1603 the Middle Border was a rather warm spot. If the King of Scots *pro tem.* wanted to take a crack at his ancient enemy the King of England, he expected the Border men to tag along. If the King of England resolved to teach his uncouth neighbour a lesson (and this happened even more frequently), the first towns to be burned were the Border towns. So, in order to maintain the enthusiasm of the Borderers for this rude form of sport, and to preserve their personal popularity in their own bailiwick, successive kings of Scotland had to think fast and often. And there began a cunning extension of the feudal system to which the Border lairds contributed their share. Grants of land were made to the Border towns on the assumption that, given a direct and permanent interest in the game, the honest burghers would join in more readily than ever. The assumption was proved to be absolutely sound. The burghs never failed to put their best men in the field, and the lands thus donated became common lands, for whose defence everyone in town was personally responsible. And when I remind you that there was in these times no Geographic Survey, and no proper method of fixing boundaries . . .

Exactly ! The riding of the marches became an annual duty for the magistrates and chief citizens, for neighbouring landlords did not hesitate to move the boundary stones and steal an acre or two. After 1603 there were no more wars, and therefore no more grants of land, but there were still landlords. So the Common Riding continued to be a big date in the calendar. And so it continues in this year of grace.

But now there is rather more to it than the riding of the marches. Thus, at Hawick, if you are a distinguished person, you may be invited to sup curds

16

and cream with the Provost and Magistrates at one of the town's farms, to spend the afternoon watching the horse racing on the town moor, and then to dance till sunrise at the Cornet's Ball. (The Cornet is the king-pin of the Common Riding—everywhere, that is, except at Selkirk; there he's the Standard-bearer. And Gala avoids the theft of either title by calling its standard-bearer the Braw Lad.) At Selkirk you will be awakened at 4 A.M. on the great day by the perambulation of a flute and drum band making antic hay with " The Girl I Left Behind Me," and when you join the crowds outbye, you will be expected to sing, regardless of the weather, " Hail, Smiling Morn." Then the Peebles ceremonies are so mixed up with survivals of the old Beltane rites that bonfires and dancing in the streets are part of the traditional fun. And naturally, everybody who can beg or hire a nag goes forth on horseback.

Of course, in Hawick (and Selkirk, Peebles, Gala-shiels, and Langholm) the land racket is a small statistic in modern economics. The prosperity of the Border burghs depends entirely on their textile trade—the manufacture of tweeds, and Cheviots, and saxonies, and serges, and worsteds, and hosiery, and the rest—but many of the citizens sit prettily in a saddle. The consequence is that the Common Ridings are not just so much fun and games on horseback or bits of ritual that the years made splendid. These medieval exercises are part of ordinary existence. You cannot miss the fact that if there was any employment in these islands for cattle lifters and fighting men, these lads would do as pretty a job as their grandfathers ever did. And while the exquisite Border laments, " The Liltin'," " The Flo'ers o' the Forest," and all the others were written for the old battles and old sorrows, there have been greater wars since Flodden with Border men in every one of them—which is, perhaps, as much as need be said of the towns of the Middle Border.

The uprush of tourists, and chain stores, and talking pictures, and radio, and Morris-Oxford English has not affected the citizens so much as you'd notice, although unfortunately they cannot be expected to resist for ever. Heavens, no ! The Border towns become more easily accessible every year. Presently, I suppose, they will look like little bits of Leeds and London. But so far, the big hill ranges have saved them from direct contact with the worst influences of modern industrialism. They are not large (indeed, they are mercifully small), and they have a cheerful vigorous life of their own. Architecturally they are not remarkable, but no one need lament that fact : the natives have had their fill of sensational architecture. Abbotsford is a pretty fair example of what can happen when romanticism and personal ambition get out of hand. (Which is no sort of criticism of Sir Walter Scott as novelist, poet, lawyer, or parent, but a purely personal comment on the only mansion on Tweedside which the casual tourist ever takes time to see.) But Abbotsford belongs to none of the towns : it is a country house, if not exactly countrified. I never think of it except as a museum.

And if you'd join me, I'd prefer to show you the Border hamlets—Swinton and its village green, Yetholm and the old haunts of the gipsies, Bowden with its lovely little thirteenth-century church, Midlem's white-washed cottages, Newcastleton whose older name is Copshawholm, or Gretna where runaway marriages are still contracted over the anvil. Or we might take a week to " do " the Abbeys, the four marvellous medieval churches that man, though he did his worst, has never quite destroyed. Better still, we might put on clean linen and attend a kennel meet of the Duke of Buccleuch's foxhounds (which means a trip to St Boswells village) or of the Dumfriesshire Hunt at Lockerbie.

There, you might say, the old aristocracy and the new meet and almost mingle, for hunting (like war) is the great leveller. And there you may see the feudal lairds and their tenants assembled in utmost amity, and exchanging greetings with all and sundry. It is now the fashion, I know, to sneer at hunting. It might be difficult to prove that, taking a severe economic (or even moral) view of the situation, hunting is justifiable or even excusable. I am not going to try. I don't give a hoot whether it is rural philanthropy on the grand scale or another instance of grinding the faces of the poor. It means nothing to me that the existence of five packs of foxhounds (and grand packs, too) keeps the Border stiff with Dukes and Belted Earls, who otherwise would spend the winter in the Shires. But I do care enormously for the easy relationship that hunting encourages between peer and ploughman, landlord and tenant, brewer and beer-drinker. I rejoice that because of hunting the Border landscape is plotted and pieced by great stout hedges and grey stone walls instead of the infernal, hideous, and strictly utilitarian wire fence of more progressive provinces. And I am also delighted to think that so long as there are still foxhounds the old mansions that look so benignantly through ancient woods at the trippers and the charabancs will still have a wisp of smoke around the chimney head, and jobs for grooms, and strappers, and gamekeepers, and gardeners.

The old life of the Border countryside will go on ; and the snootier varieties of hunting, I might add in passing, have been practised in these parts for a thousand years. Did not the ancient Scottish kings hunt the deer with dogs in Ettrick Forest ? They did, frequently and at considerable length, and a thousand years is not so long in the history of the Border, in which it is only the modern chapter that begins with Wallace. Before he troubled us there were Agricola and some others, and the story is not ended yet. So there is hope for the hunting.

There is also, as it happens, hope for agriculture. The big farms and the little farms are mostly paying dividends again. And hope for the towns : the textile trade has revived slightly in the last two years. If this double revival continues the Border will have time and money to spend on the preservation of its soul. Meanwhile, in common with the other provinces of Scotland, it is mightily troubled by the tax-collector, and inspectors of this and that, and the inconsistencies of the drink laws ; but I do not know that the Boards of Experts, or the Minister of Agriculture, or the League of Nations will want to do much about that— or even that you will be greatly interested. I do not know how closely you will want to stick to the romantical tourist route, so that will be all for to-day. Farewell.

by

G. ROWNTREE HARVEY

How does the East of Scotland differ from the West ? Hereafter a man of the North-East tells you about the fishing communities and the inner significance of Buchan

ABERDEEN AND ALL THAT

IN every country that is fortunate enough to possess them, the east coast differs considerably from the west and the difference is seen not only in geographical features and in climate but also in the nature of the people. That is very true of Scotland, and here the differences are so clearly marked as to be surprising in a country where the distances between the seaboards are comparatively short.

When the native of Glenelg or Gairloch looks westward, he sees misty islands, near and far, and he dreams dreams and talks softly of Tir n'an Og, the island of the ever-young, that lies in the sunset of those western seas. When the characteristic man of Aberdeen looks eastward over the North Sea he thinks of trade and fishing, just as, when he looks westwards and sees the hills, he thinks of granite and the tourist traffic. Those, of course, are the superficial thoughts of the east coast man. Sea and granite have moods and hearts of deeper, more passionate quality—if you can catch those moods or get at those hearts. The man of the west, it is sometimes to be suspected, has only a heart on a sleeve and moods like the mist on his hills and islands.

The history and legality of Edinburgh ; the foreign trade of Leith ; the jute of Dundee ; the granite of

Aberdeen ; the little conglomerate trades of Inverness
—create differences on the east coast that are almost
as great as the differences in speech and character of
their peoples. But for a greater part of its length, the
east coast of Scotland is not divided in its folk, but
still to some degree united by one calling—alas, now in
its decline in those communities—where unity was once
both internal and external, and strong.

These were, of course, the fishing villages. From
Eyemouth to Avoch (call the latter " Auch " when you
speak its name) you would have found—and in many
cases, thank goodness, will still find—folk who have
the same ways and customs, the same superstitions
and prejudices, the same garb on both male and
female, the same turns of speech and a likeness in
accent.

How deeply these characteristics are inherent in
the fisher-folk is best to be found, for instance, in such
suburban communities as those of Footdee and Torry,
at Aberdeen. At Torry, the growing Granite City—
now more and more being built of brick and concrete
rather than of silver granite—has encompassed the old
fishing village with ramparts of villas and council
houses and bungalows ; but within old Torry, with its
little houses, its wooden jetties, its brown-sailed yawls
and home-made nets, the life of the centuries goes on
quietly, though not so evenly now, perhaps, as once
on a day when steam and the trawlers were something
new, strange and strongly objected to, even to the
extent of minor riots and stone-throwing.

In Torry and Footdee you will hear the lovely lilt
of the fisher speech ; you will still see the women in
dark blue serge skirts, with many tucks, caught up to
show wincey petticoats ; you will still see the boys

and men in dark blue guernseys and dark blue trousers. As in all the fishing villages, at least of the north-east coast, there are only half-a-dozen or more surnames for the whole community; "tee" names are still in use to distinguish different families of the same name— "Rosie," "Dosie," "Crab," "Rockie" and so on. Children are still called by peculiar diminutives and their father's or mother's Christian names added by way of a distinguishing prefix. So we have "Wullie's Jeannikie," and "Annie's Jimmikie," and this may be carried on even into a third generation, such as "Mary's Wullie's Johnnikie."

There is among such communities a complete lore of the weather, of course, and there are curious superstitions, such as the banning of the mention of the word "pig." In school the children will, while attempting to hide the fact, cross their fingers if the teacher mentions the forbidden word. I have heard of one village where on a day a pig broke loose and ran down the single street. That day not a single boat put out to sea !

And so far as the fish and their curing are concerned, there were villages where a certain method of treating the fish brought fame and comparative fortune. Even southerners talk of "finnan haddie," though it is known in North-east Scotland as "yellow fish." How many of these southerners know that this particular brand of smoked fish takes its name from the tiny village of Findon on the Kincardine coast where the smoked haddock had either its origin or its greatest vogue— Findon—Fin'on— "finnan?" From Collieston on the Aberdeenshire, or Buchan, coast came another form of tastily-cured fish—"Speldin's"; this time, however, with only a local vogue.

To show how the old and the new may meet—if you travel by the morning train from Arbroath to Kirkcaldy, or vice-versa by the evening train, you will encounter at Arbroath a sudden incursion of fisher-folk, men and women, with baskets of fish which will be sold in town and village and countryside of Angus and Fife during that day. The women still wear the characteristic dress of serge and wincey, with a blue cotton apron added ; and they are also the last wearers of the bustle. The bustle, however, is not worn for fashion's sake, but to balance the weight of the creel (or basket) in which are " caller haddies." Once inside and settled in their carriages, the fisher lassies from Arbroath produce their packets of cigarettes and their packs of cards, and the journey is spent in " puffing " and playing. The talk will be of dances and films, but the accent and lilt is still that of the grandfathers and grandmothers whom the " fags " and the " cartes " would shock abominably, even although both grandmother and grandfather might have mightily liked a puff at their cutty pipes !

In another aspect the fisher-folk are strongly and often emotionally religious. Periodic " revivals " break out, especially in the north and north-east, and the evangelical mission and the Methodist Church have always had their strongholds in the fishing village. I remember as a youngster being present in the Methodist church of a large eastern seaport where that religion had become staid, if none the less staunch. On this evening there was present a band of Methodists from the Moray fishing villages, and I, perhaps more than the usual members of the congregation, accustomed to such occasional visits, was utterly startled during the first prayer when the fishermen broke in with loud

DESIGN FROM YESTERDAY: A Highland Inn by the Roadside

DESIGN FROM YESTERDAY : Dundarave—A Fortified House

Design from Yesterday : A Corner of the Garden

Design from Yesterday: Swanston—A Lowland Village

and perfervid " Hallelujah ! " " Amen to that, brother ! "
" Praise the Lord ! " But even the ordinary members
of the congregation looked, I thought, just a little
embarrassed by such riches of feeling.

So much for the folk ; what of the places of the
east coast ? Well, beginning at the south, and in
face of possible protests, I have always thought that
the first stretch from Berwick to the mouth of the
Forth, with the exception of the older villages, is not
too interesting.

When we approach the Forth estuary it is not only
the more interesting coast-line but history that begins
to take hold on us. Between Dunfermline toun and
Edinburgh toun lies that storied stretch of water.
Think of it only in terms of shipping and you will see
a procession that begins, so far as we know, with the
coracles of the saints and can be temporarily ended
with the surrendered German Fleet. To and fro, to
and fro, across the Forth have come and gone kings
and queens and courtiers, bound for heaven, bound
for marriage, coronation or the block. Scottish poets
from Henryson and Dunbar to Burns and Stevenson
have moved upon its waters or been moved by them
—to song.

But that is the trouble about the Forth—we are all
so concerned with what has been about it and what is
now in and above it, that we are apt to forget the
Forth itself. Visitors nowadays are sent only to look
at or cross the railway bridge—there is also a road
bridge now—and marvel, at the bridge only. It is
long since I cast my penny into the Forth on my first
journey across the greater bridge—what a copper
harvest must lie there !—and the marvel of the bridge
is merely subconscious with me now. More to me on

my journeys and sojournings over and about the Forth are the ever-changing beauties of the estuary and its romantic shores.

They will tell you that only the poor or unsophisticated can find any pleasure on Forthside from Kirkcaldy to Queensferry ; it is so spoiled, they say, by commerce in action and decay. I have not found it so—perhaps I am unsophisticated as well as poor— and have spent many happy hours watching the waters when they looked like a pavement of violets, when they were as lapis lazuli, or even when they were slaty-green and flecked by the little white caps that indicate to bad sailors the particular *mal* of this particular *mer*. And always, from the Fife side, is one of the great romantic views of Scotland—when you can see it —the truly Auld Reekie and Arthur's Seat.

Passing Kirkcaldy, let us strike inland so that we may approach the Fife villages as they should be approached, by the white roads that wind between the miles of flat green fields. On the way we have looked at Largo and remembered Alexander Selkirk and " The Boatie Rows " ; at Lundin we have remembered that golf in Fife exists outside St Andrews. But now the road goes east, and northward along the coast we see the church spires or towers and the roofs of the higher-set houses of Elie, St Monance, Pittenweem, Anstruther and Crail. Dunfermline belongs to history and the Carnegie Trust ; St Andrews to culture, history and golf ; Cupar to the law ; Markinch to whiskey ; Ladybank to coal ; but the coast villages belong to simply happy holidaymakers, and the artists. Just as Iona in the west has been over-painted in recent years, so have these Fifeshire coast places. They're worth it, but it may do them various kinds of harm in the end ; colour and quaintness may endure for a time, but . . .

And so, by Kingsbarns, to St Andrews, a town which, apart from golf and a certain air of snobbishness in certain quarters that can be completely neglected, is one of the most enchanting, not only in Scotland, but, I venture, the world. In Scotland's Oxford, history surges again upon you—Wishart and Knox and Cardinal Beaton, these three are sufficient out of multitudes to suggest a heroic and highly-coloured past. If you know nought of them, the gentleman who swings the lantern round the bottle dungeon in the castle will chant a lurid tale for you of other parts of St Andrews' past.

Along the sands and just round the corner lies the Firth of Tay, and, across the water yonder, that is Dundee, best seen at a distance, backed by the redundantly named Law Hill. For me, Dundee and the Tay mean the lovely prospect that lies south-west of the town and, strictly speaking, on the north side of the river, the many-hued Carse of Gowrie. Summer or winter there's beauty there, one of the loveliest gateways to the inner beauties of Scotland.

North now by Angus, with sands for its seashore— loveliest at Lunan Bay—and red loam below its grass and corn. The sea and that red loam undoubtedly produce the douce, half-Sassenach, half-Celtic Angus man, a Scottish type that has yet to find its true portrayer in Scottish literature. Barrie did a little, but London, as always, spoiled the truth ; Violet Jacob began, but has never finished, her portrait.

The red loam and the sands and the men continue halfway into Kincardine. But by the time the county capital is reached, the coast becomes rockbound and the Aberdeenshire influence is stronger. Stonehaven is another haunt of artists and holidaymakers, a miniature Genoa, rising in terraces from the sea. See it at morning when the sun is just over the sea-rim and the first smoke spirals are rising from chimney pots, red, white and black.

See Aberdeen, too, at morning, from the sea—pure Greek it is thus and then, a granite Aphrodite, a white body touched to warmer beauty by the rosy touch of dawn. Her toes are to the sea, and on either side a river runs. As you move up the mouth of the River Dee to the harbour the Greek romance of the distance gives way to the not entirely inartistic aspect of modernism—painter and etcher of to-day could find subjects ready to hand here. But as you enter the harbour, again you have a town that begins in terraces, and on the plateau are ranged a great host of towers, white granite and dark freestone—a city of worshippers? Well, one thing Aberdonians do worship, as a great part of the world knows, is the appearance of their town, and rightly. After the town, Aberdonians venerate and encourage the legend of their character. Hard as their granite, frugal to meanness, yet, as every visitor soon finds out, though they be hard externally Aberdeen is no mean city, but gives freely to good causes and enjoys life all the more because its inhabitants know how to save for their enjoyment and leave something in the cupboard, and the bank, for the morning.

Harbour, fish - market, granite - yards, factories, churches, schools and an ancient university—these make up the life and living of Aberdeen. It is a city that does not forget ever that it belongs to the most ancient of days in Scottish history, although most of its inhabitants are content with the pride and let even knowledge of the history go.

The raiding northmen came here when the settlement was known as Apardion ; Mary of Scots was compelled to watch the execution of one of her lovers on its *grande place* ; a Scottish saint, Machar, founded its cathedral, which still exists ; and an uncanonised saint, Bishop William Elphinstone, one of the greatest men of medieval Scotland, founded its university and was the " onlie begetter " of two of the loveliest pieces of Scottish architecture and church decoration, both of which still exist in King's College Chapel.

Aberdeen is the southernmost point and the Aberdonian the urban counterpart of Buchan and its natives.

What is Buchan ? It is both an idea and an actuality. In actuality it is the coast of Aberdeenshire and some ten to fifteen miles inland. The first part of that coast consists of miles of golden sands, and at one part, Forvie, those sands are said to cover a buried village or town—one of the few romantic aspects of that coast. Then come rocks of fierceness and treachery for shipping. Inland the acres are comparatively bare, miles of rolling farmland and here and there a little hill. To be told that fugitives after Culloden in the '45 hid in Buchan is to wonder how they managed it.

Buchan men partake of their rock and their landscape, and so does their speech. The character of the people of Buchan is somewhat hard and rugged to those accustomed to the softer type of southern Scot, and their dialect as unintelligible as the Gaelic of the Celt. But it is pure old speech that has its kin, in Britain, among the Northumbrians and Yorkshiremen ; over the North Sea, among the Scandinavians, the

Germans, the Dutch and the Flemings of Belgium. In character as well as speech the "Buchaner" resembles the Flemings, more especially those of the hinterland of Antwerp, the Campine.

Not for nothing was there in medieval times a strong connection between Aberdeen and Aberdeenshire and the Flemings. Scotland and France still speak of the Auld Alliance, but this other was an older alliance. From Campvere and Bruges the people of the east coast brought not only the exchange of trade but knowledge of the finer things of life—apparel, furniture, the adornment of churches, art. Aberdeen in the Middle Ages was a centre of religious drama, and its best known, but lost, play was "The Haly Blude." Bruges's best known church is the Chapelle du Saint Sang. Is there any connection? And it was only right when Aberdeen produced the first British artist of note, George Jamesone, that he should learn the craft of his art in Antwerp.

But few Flemings were, and are, artists, and so is it with the men of Aberdeen and Buchan. They are nearer the Flemings in their industry, in making the most of bare acres—and they have made much, in driving a hard bargain, in a seeming taciturnity alleviated with bursts of rough joviality, in making a little money and speech go a long way, in a certain amount of unorthodoxy in the matter of the moral code. They have been sometimes alleged to be, not exactly not men of their word, but next door to it. There is, however, no doubt that they are "bonnie fechters," as the Germans of 1914-18 could tell. What also cannot be doubted is that they are a race of men in most ways unique in Scotland.

At Peterhead, which is the real capital of Buchan,

we come to the former home of the whalers, and at
Fraserburgh in sight of the Moray Firth. All along
the coast now are fishing villages, with one town, Banff.
We come to Moray proper at Spey Bay, and here on
sea and land is beauty of a softer kind than the
Aberdeenshire coast can offer. Across the firth we
look to the far, dim shores of Ross and Cromarty, and
Moray Firth sunsets are almost as famous as those of
the west of Scotland. Inland the fields of Moray,
known as the Laigh, are softly coloured and rich in
their production.

At Nairn, speech begins to soften until, at Inverness,
it reaches a quality as unusual in its sound as that of
Buchan is in its words and sound. But Inverness lies
so far inland and belongs so much more to the highlands
than the coast that, though unwillingly, we pass it by.

Round Tarbat Ness to Dornoch, Golspie, Brora,
Helmsdale, Lybster, Wick, and so to John o' Groats—
for long along that coast hills and the sea meet, and
we have a people that are neither Celt nor Sassenach.
Bit by bit we are reaching out to the islands of Orkney
and Shetland, and across the North Sea to Scandinavia.
Thoughts of the northmen and the wreck of the Armada
are mingled in the backlands of our minds. Because of
their situation, here is a people strong in individuality,
untouched to a great extent by southern influences.

And so to John o' Groats, for most people a
geographical name only, the top end of a tour of
Britain—the opposite to Land's End—the starting-
place for rallying motorists who may or may not land
eventually in Monte Carlo—curious opposite to the
lighthouse settlement of Duncansbay Head, to all that
is Scottish east coast. . . .

If eyes could see as far as the distance from John o'

Groats to Berwick, they would still be intercepted by that jutting shoulder of Buchan. There is more in that than geographical conformation. That accords with other matters in a survey of the Scottish east coast. Buchan is more than an intercepter; it is one of Scotland's strongest bulwarks against alien invasion in speech and character; it is the essence of Scottish east coast. Its individuality may outlast the " Sassenach-ing " of the Gael; it may still be Scotland when all the rest is completely anglicised. That process is well under weigh. And what is the surest way of judging opposition to it? Wireless programmes. The Gael and the " Buchaner " are specially catered for by the British Broadcasting Corporation. Yet look at the extent of Gaeldom compared with Buchan.

But how that Buchan shoulder juts !

by
ALASTAIR BORTHWICK

Do you like your Highlands neat?
If so, Mr Borthwick tells you where
and when to go and what to take
with you. There is also a charming
digression on Glen Arnisdale

TWENTY MILES A DAY IN THE WEST

A DOCTOR of science, whose job it was to know these things, once told me that three-quarters of Scotland was under woods, deer-forests, or rough grazing ; and if you combine that piece of information with the fact that more than half the population of the country lives in the narrow plain between the Clyde and the Forth, you may reasonably conclude that walking in Scotland differs from walking in the south of England, where it is practically impossible to be farther than one mile from a bar parlour. Actually, there are many places in Scotland, and you need not go far out of your way to find them, where the nearest roof is ten miles away, and thatched at that. Also, there are mountains.

This need not discourage the less energetic walker. Anyone prepared to travel ten miles in a day on the flat of his feet can see most that is best of Scotland and sleep in a bed at night. On ten miles a day you can make friends with shepherds and gamekeepers, and know places where there is neither road nor living soul in sight, which is a highly desirable state of affairs. But it seems to me that Scotland is specially adapted for those who can stretch the ten miles to fifteen or twenty as a matter of course, and the twenty to twenty-five or thirty in an emergency. The little extra energy opens up country and walking peculiar to Scotland alone.

Take, for example, the Highlands of the North-West, a tract of country as big as Wales, known in a vague sort of way to most inhabitants of the British Isles as a place where rich people go to shoot grouse. Stand on any mountain there, and you will see, as far as the horizon, mountains and still more mountains, heaped up on each other, jumbled, a wilderness more perpendicular than horizontal. But look at a map of the North-West, and you will see order in it. The mountains lie in long, loosely connected ridges, and between each ridge and its neighbour runs a glen. And all the ridges and all the glens run roughly in the same direction. This is important. The " grain " of the North-West Highlands runs approximately north-east to south-west.

Civilisation does here exactly what it does in any other mountainous region—it follows the glens, where earth has silted down from the mountains and crops can be grown. So your ten-miles-a-day walker has only to follow the glens and he will find roofs and fires and food. Also, he will walk on roads—rough ones, probably, but roads just the same.

But the man who prefers something more energetic is not tied to walking perpetually either north-east or south-west. He can do what the drovers did in the days when there were more substantial things in the Highlands to drive than grouse—take to the old tracks which connect glen with glen, over the passes which cut north and south through the mountains ; start up through the birch trees, cross the bald crest above the tree-line, and drop down into a new world on the other side. It may be that it is sheer perversity to leave the roads, for they are beautiful ; but travelling against the grain has its beauties too. It is always attractive to choose a route of your own instead of following someone else's nose. It is good to feel utterly dependent on your own efforts, with no motor cars to destroy the illusion. And moreover, to cross a pass and look down on the other side was a source of satisfaction to mankind long before Moses saw Canaan.

It is this possibility of independence which gives Scotland, in spite of its scope for easy-going, short-distance walking, its still further scope for walking of a more exciting kind. There are hundreds of not too inaccessible glens, dotted here and there with Baedecker three-star beauty-spots ; but between them and beyond them are stretches of country, ranging from the starkly grand all the way to the pure grocer's calendar, where an occasional shepherd's cottage is the most you can hope for. Carried to extremes (and extremes are acquired tastes) a liking for such places can lead to real adventure. Two friends of mine, for instance, spent last Easter crossing the Cairngorms—walking country, judged by summer standards. They slept in a windproof tent, melted snow for water, never saw so much as a sheep or trod on anything but windpacked snow for three days, and lived in the same way and faced much the same problems as an Arctic expedition.

That is the extreme case ; but between it and ten miles a day lie a thousand less Spartan alternatives —like, for argument's sake, Glen Arnisdale.

You start from the Great Glen, where the Loch Ness Monster lives during the tourist season, and strike towards the sea along Glengarry. And when you have walked for a day and most of the next day you come to a place where the road, which has been crawling upwards ever since you started, tumbles over a cliff and expires at the bottom, killed, apparently, by the fall. This place where the road stops is called Kinloch Hourn, which means the Head of the Loch of Hell, and looks like it. There is apparently no way out except by the road you have just descended ; but if you look hard enough you will see a stalker's track struggling up the hill on the other side of the glen. It is excessively steep. Nevertheless, follow it ; and as your eyebrows grow heavy with sweat, draw solace from the fact that the top is only a few hundred feet away and that there is something very much worth seeing on the other side.

Behind me, the first time I crawled over that pass and saw the mist rise and dissolve and the sun come out, was a long day of bleak moors and peat hags, where the tops of the mountains gleamed as the rain streamed down their smooth rock slabs ; and there was rock again where the road pitched down to Kinloch Hourn, rock worn to the bone by ancient glaciers. And then the dismal plod up the stalker's track. And then Glen Arnisdale.

Now that I know how it ends, I would not have it any other way. I would not even abate by one rank whiff the smell of seaweed long decayed on the shore of Hourn. I would not have it otherwise, because Nature in the North-West manages her contrasts skilfully, offsets her Hamlet with a comic grave-digger, heightens her comedy with a hint of tragedy. The moors, and bogs, and rock which precede that pass are only the black velvet which shows off the diamond, for Glen Arnisdale is green, and wooded, and altogether delightful. There are birds in its trees, and trout in its lochans, and red deer where the mountains plunge down through the birches. There are rabbits in the bracken, and, because there are rabbits, weasels hunting in line, nose to tail. Thanks to Landseer and his contemporaries, the Highlands still live in the popular imagination as a uniformly grey landscape with two cows and an acre of bog in front of a mountain mainly obscured by mist. The conception of the Highlands as a monochrome steel engraving dies hard. These artists never used the bright red of Glen Arnisdale's autumn bracken, or the delicate green of its birch trees in spring. And, with their obsession for mist, they forgot the whole point of the North-West Highlands, which is the clearness of the air on those days when the wind is in the west and the cloud-shadows are chasing each other across the mountain-sides, the clearness which brings out the trees, and rocks, and the ripples on the lochans crisp and sharp.

You can see all that in Glen Arnisdale, tucked away and lost in a pocket in the mountains. There is a path of sorts through the lower part of the glen, but that dies before it climbs to the head, just as the stalker's track dies before it quite descends to it. Behind you is the solid wall you have just climbed, cutting you off from Hourn and the moors. In front are nine miles of winding, wooded glen before you reach the gamekeeper's cottage at Inverarnisdale, with a sunset thrown in for good measure, sliding into the sea beyond the peaks of Skye.

That is only one of hundreds of glens in the Highlands, all different, all with that little something which gives them personalities of their own. Glen Arnisdale happens to be my choice. You may think differently. You may prefer something fluffier, like Glen Affric, with its birch forest ; or something grander, like Glen Nevis or the Larig Ghru ; or something both spectacular and accessible, like Glencoe. You may prefer the pines of Speyside to the birches of the Mallaig road, the barren grandeur of Sutherland to the Rothiemurchus Forest. Or you may prefer the Outer Isles, where there are no trees at all. These are things for the individual taste. You must make your own choice.

But before you do so, consider that section of Scotland which lies south of the central industrial belt. If your tastes lie in the direction of solitude, you might do worse than visit Galloway and explore the rolling hills and moors that lie between the coast and Loch Ken, where the heather and rough grass and bracken roll mile after mile, and there are resounding names like Meikle Bin, the Dungeon of Buchan, and Clatteringshaws. Or follow the Border valleys and drove roads, where there are sheep in the fields and in the hills, and stout market towns, and ancient castles, fertile country farmed and built upon for centuries so that it is smooth and ordered.

When you have made your choice, consider ways and means. Equipment for walking in Scotland is much the same as it is anywhere else, though it might be as well to remember that there is a Gaelic proverb which says : " On a good day, take your cloak. On a wet day, please yourself." But there are four points worth bearing in mind—the Scottish Youth Hostel Association, the Forestry Commission, the magnetic north pole, and the curious habits of shooting tenants.

The Youth Hostel Association has chains of hostels, some extremely comfortable, some just comfortable, scattered up and down the country, so arranged that they are within one day's march of each other. A small fee makes you a member, and a shilling a night gives you a roof over your head, a bed and blankets to sleep in, and a kitchen and pots and pans to cook in. If you want either luxury or cooked meals, you will have to go elsewhere ; but if you want good company, I can recommend them. Or you may prefer hotels. In the Highlands they are frequently so far apart that a hotel walking tour would be difficult to plan in many of the best districts ; but almost anywhere you can use wayside cottages as links. Or you can use cottages exclusively.

The Forestry Commission is a small point, but an important one. The Commission owns large tracts of land, all of it fenced and all of it marked by a distinctive notice-board ; and its foresters are apt to be rude to people who light bonfires on, or trample over, young trees. They disapprove of people who are careless with their cigarette-ends. They are also prone to giving advice and passing the time of day pleasantly with people who do none of these things.

The uses of the magnetic north pole are not sufficiently realised by people who walk. Walkers in the south of England can rest secure in the knowledge that either " The Green Man " or " The Pig and Whistle " is within hailing distance ; but walkers in the more lonely parts of Scotland most definitely can not, and they have only themselves to thank if the mist comes down and they have no compass. Most walkers carry a map, but a map without a compass in mist is about as useful as a kite without a tail. If you intend keeping to the roads, do as you like. A compass will be of very little use to you. But if you intend to take to the hills or go across country, take a compass. You can buy a perfectly good one for a couple of shillings. In mid-summer it may save you an annoying night out : in mid-winter it may save your life.

I mentioned maps. There are several available, mostly good ; but the best are those issued by the Ordnance Survey. They are accurate and legible. If you keep to roads, the half-inch to the mile edition will give you all you want, and will serve fairly comfortably off the roads as well. For cross-country or hill walking, take the one-inch-to-the-mile edition. There is a section of either to cover the district you want.

Then there is the shooting question. The Highland landlord has come in for a good deal of abuse, but on the whole he is a reasonable fellow and much less given to throwing his weight about than he was twenty years ago. There are ill-bred exceptions to this rule ; but mostly the man who shoots deer and grouse need not trouble you if you remember a few dates and exercise a little ordinary common sense.

The first date—the twelfth of August—everybody knows. The grouse shooting starts then. The second date is less generally known. It is not a fixed one, but ranges from the tail-end of August through the first half of September, and is the opening of the deer-stalking season, which continues through September and finishes with the hind shooting from October to Christmas. Also, landlords are apt to be touchy about their grouse for at least a month before the shooting actually opens. You must be prepared to meet with opposition on the hills from early July until late October, or even later.

In actual practice, there is seldom any trouble for the walker in July ; but from August onwards there frequently is. Stalkers can be surprisingly disgruntled at the end of a five-hour crawl through the heather when a total stranger comes between them and their stag ; and they are even less inclined to be friendly if the stranger has reached that point via the estate's holy of holies, the deer sanctuary. Five minutes spent in a sanctuary by a hiker may scare every deer in the place on to the estate next door for a matter of a week.

Go warily, therefore, while the stalking is on. Gamekeepers and stalkers are as fond of a chat as most people, and it is the easiest thing in the world to drop in on them in the early morning and ask where they intend stalking that day. If the man is friendly, he will tell you where you may cross his estate without disturbing game. If the man is not friendly there is no harm done, and you may have the luck to learn where you can trespass with the least chance of being caught. And if the worst comes to the worst, no one can keep you off a public road.

There is only one more point. In the Central Highlands and the southern half of Scotland there are few very reliable rules about the weather ; but in the North-West and the Inner Hebrides there are. If you intend going west or north of the Great Glen, go in May, June, or September. You will find these months drier than July or August.

The rest is common sense.

THE CITIES AND THEIR CITIZENS

by
JAMES BRIDIE

Scotland has her " lovelies " and her
Socialites. Are they an aristocracy?
And if so what do they mean? Here
a distinguished dramatist examines the
leaders of our urban communities

URBAN MANNERS AND CUSTOMS

BEFORE I begin this short survey it will be
necessary, for comparison's sake, to give an
account of society in Southern England. There
has been a steady drift north of publications and ideas
from that quarter for many years. Of late the British
Broadcasting Company has made us very familiar with
its spoken idiom. We cannot evite it. It is with
us, and its habits and manners as it lives insistently
demand comparison with our own.

Society in South England is very strongly organised.
It is organised on the hierarchical system. Everybody
knows exactly the state to which it has pleased God to
call him and is, on the whole, content with that state.
He knows his place, as they say. It is understood that
a gasfitter's wife goes in to dinner before a grocer's
wife, or vice versa. It is realised that neither of them
may expect to go to dinner at all (except in public)
with a stockbroker's wife. Every grade is recognised
from a brahmin to an untouchable. This grading is
never spoken about among what are called the best
people. It is hidden by a democratic veil and lied
about if necessary. It is part of the Englishman's
Secret Religion and helps to make the English the
happiest, safest and most contented people on earth.
They are never distressed by irrelevant heart-burnings.

45

Attempts are often made to disturb this fixed social scale, but never with any success. Thus, newspaper proprietors are made into Lords ; but the word " newspaper " is always understood when their titles are mentioned. Every errand boy knows that a Newspaper Lord is no more a real Lord (*i.e.* the descendant of a King's mistress, favourite or money-lender) than a Law Lord in Scotland is a Real Lord.

In revenge for this—for it is a pity to spend so much money on an inferior article—the newspapers have invented or collected a group of people and called them, amusingly, Socialites and their group, Society. Its doings are chronicled and pictured and its composition is determined largely by the amount of money its members are foolish and vulgar enough to spend on personal advertisement. It follows that the chronicles of this " Society " give a general effect of folly and vulgarity. They are salted from time to time with the names and doings of really important brahmins, for the habit of horsewhipping Editors has lapsed a little in recent years ; and provincials like ourselves are apt to be misled. We do not see the invisible markings on the forehead. Indeed, this deliberately false picture of the upper reaches of the English hierarchy might have sophisticated * the whole fabric if the Cinema had not come to its rescue.

The Hollywood Colonials have already completely defeated the attempt to found a sensational, irresponsible spectacular " Society " in Mayfair, London, England. They are more interesting to the gossip readers in every way. They are more extravagant, more vulgar, and, when it comes to being photographed, they are, of course, professionals. It takes a lot of reiteration to

---

* *Sophisticated :* Rendered spurious by admixture. *Vide* Dictionary.

46

persuade us that some haggard little rat of a woman is a leading beauty on the strength of a hideous series of all too accurate photographs in the weekly press. On the other hand, the divine guttersnipes of Los Angeles *are* leading beauties. They look it. They are paid for it. And their impresarios take care that we are not allowed to forget it. The poor wretched local " lovelies " are crowded into the back pages among the underwear advertisements and, even there, they are outshone by the mannequins. As for their parties and their general behaviour it now excites no interest at all. A trousered, spectacled bunch of Socialites in a snow-storm cannot be compared for news value with a crowd of sightly stars sporting in an agate swimming pool in costumes our emaciated lovelies dare not wear.

So the English hierarchy is steady again. The bejewelled sweepers have themselves been swept under the wardrobe out of sight and the Throne itself is suitably surrounded by ladies and gentlemen.

In Scotland, there is no hierarchy. The attempts of the newspapers to create a Society have always been a little pathetic. Even in the North, where the clan system provided a sort of primitive aristocracy, the reputation of the Chief has become so bad that his prestige has followed it into oblivion—for the High-landers are a kindly race. Two or three Highland Chiefs survive and assert a sort of authority. A few more are treated by their subjects with the sort of affectionate regard they give to the village idiot. But the MacHoochaye of MacHoochaye, take him by and large, cuts no ice and butters no parsnips.

The Lowlanders have always been democratic. On the Borders, for a time, they grouped themselves under a few formidable ruffians for cattle-stealing enterprises and the like ; but, if the ruffians' sons were not so big and brutal as their fathers, they made short work of them. It was all a purely utilitarian arrangement and had nothing to do with aristocracy as the Englishman understands it. From the Reformation onwards our Nobles have had to do exactly as they are told and have always been touchingly anxious to please. Even their servants have a habit of arrogance towards them. They have to show pleasing individual characteristics before they are allowed so much as to open a bazaar or speak at a Burns Supper. Their rank is but the guinea stamp and the guinea is out of currency.

Now it is well known that Society, as an organisation, is formed by a small number of people inducing a large number of people to work for them and their dependents. Whether this small number call themselves an aristocracy, a theocracy, a plutocracy or, more simply, the State, they are, and insist on being, the head stone of the corner. No organised society has ever existed without these energetic and acquisitive beings. What is the Corner Stone, the Governing Class in Scotland, and what is their manner of life ?

Scotland is divided into one swollen city, three large ones, a number of considerable towns, an agricultural area, a fishing area, and a large playground. The bloated city and its ancillary towns account for nearly a third of the whole population, and Edinburgh, Dundee and Aberdeen for another sixth, so that half of the inhabitants of Scotland are city-dwellers. The bulk and compactness of this lump of humanity suggests that when we speak of Scotland " doing " anything we must consider that the preponderating motive force comes from the cities and, to be quite plain about it, from Glasgow.

The Capital City, however, is Edinburgh, and it is to it we must look first for the social graces and arts which are the criteria of a civilised nation. The principal industries of Edinburgh are Law and Religion and, in the absence or defaulting of a hereditary ruling class, these activities, one might think, would provide us with capable substitutes. They even traditionally comfort and support the hereditary branch of the ruling class, and it is for this reason that the priest and the lawyer are so often targets for revolutionary bullets after their patrons have fled.

I am afraid we must regretfully admit that the corner stone is not in Edinburgh. Take them for all in all, the lawyers are a queasy, shabby lot, nothing like the fine whales and porpoises who used to wallow in seas of port and claret in the great days of the Capital. As for the Clergy, they have lost their Hell and have a very nerveless hold on the Absolute. The General Assembly itself is given over to skippers and dancers and dalliers with dames. The dames themselves, if we are to judge from the Woman's Column in the daily papers, are a sore declension on the old. These columns are bloodless. There is neither a lusty sinfulness nor a militant righteousness from end to end of them ; and wit, which grows luxuriantly wherever great ladies are, is never found. We must conclude that the talk of the ladies of Edinburgh is graceless gabble and their deeds are naught.

At one time Edinburgh was a literary centre or, at least, a centre of literary criticism the ferocity of which was feared throughout the three Kingdoms. Literature depends even more than the Church and the Bar on patronage. There is no literature in Edinburgh now. There is no art either. If a Raeburn still lives there, he has no chubby, confident, princely people to

49 D

paint. The high places of the city are full of Watsonians —chubby, yes ; confident, moderately ; but princely, no.

Let us turn our attention to Glasgow. Surely there we shall find a vigorous plutocracy at least. The men who made the Clyde had surely sufficient energy left over to make sons and daughters. In their spare time they commissioned many noble buildings and parks and galleries and concert halls and theatres. They chose great men to teach in their University and used them worthily. In one sphere at least of the arts, in painting on canvas, they made Glasgow a little Paris. Portraits by Guthrie, Lavery and Henry show us that they were represented by splendid, solid-looking Bailies. Here were the makings of a grand Merchant City, like Carthage, like Venice. Did it so develop ? It did not.

Glasgow is a slum-suburb of Dublin. Its Merchant Princes, with all their gifts, were never gentry. The beautiful, tatterdemalion city of Dublin is haunted by ghosts. Honour and dishonour stand together in her streets. Neither of these strange conceptions is to be found in Glasgow. Gentility stained and battered keeps still its own loveliness ; but decency destroyed is another thing. The best Glasgow could ever claim was decency. Decency and indecency stand together in her streets.

The dog, the Scriptures tell us, will return to its vomit again, and the sow, from being washed, to wallowing in the mire. This hard saying has its comfortable aspect. The dog may again be cleansed in its inward parts and the sow in its outward. There do not want signs that Glasgow is conscious of its state and is making ready to remedy it. The grandsons of the men who made the Clyde are coming back from their English public schools and colleges, with pretty clothes and mincing accents it is true, but also with some of the sense of responsibility that made the Empire. The intermediate generation, who left the smelly purlieus for places where they could solace their souls with hunting, shooting, fishing and pursuing golf, actually did their part too. The people who worked for them, finding a vacuum where their lords should have been, began to consider whether they might not do a little bit for themselves. They took the step of electing a proletarian Corporation. Glasgow found, somewhat to her surprise, that those who had been nasty demagogues in opposition proved themselves in office to be as responsible, more enterprising, and probably less corrupt than their predecessors in office. And the sense of sin, one may imagine, is strong within them. The state of Glasgow society is not hopeless. Those who are making it, however, are not themselves a corner stone. They are scavengers. There is a great deal to be dug away before the outlines of the arch appear. We can but hope that irrelevant imbecilities about Marxism and Capitalism will not divert their attention and that a civic sense will grow again. When that day comes we shall have people and places to respect and we shall be as nearly happy as it is possible to be. We shall have a stable society.

It will be a society peculiarly suited to a democracy like Scotland. When I say democracy, I do not mean the method of counting fat heads and then pretending to abide by the decision so reached. I mean the State in which every individual is a King. By that test we are not a democracy yet.

I suppose the truth is that we are boiling up again and must wait for a bit before we are "jelled." I may be wrong in thinking that the community nearest to our ultimate shape is to be found in Aberdeen.

by
A. D. MACKIE

Though Edinburgh is a capital from which some of the glory has vanished, it retains something of a royal air, and one of her lively natives here shows you how to enjoy the pleasures she can offer you

THE PLEASURES OF EDINBURGH

HISTORICAL, romantic, literary, legendary Edinburgh is for the visitor, rather than for those who were born and reared in the place. Just as, I am told, the people of Pisa treat their renowned Leaning Tower with marked disrespect, the citizens of Edinburgh are relatively unmoved by the thousand and one things over which a visitor might go into ecstasies. With the exception of the professional guides, cabmen, charabanc-drivers, and the street urchins who shoot out at you from dingy alleys and bawl in your ears a rigmarole about the buildings and monuments, which is really a roundabout way of asking for baksheesh, the people of Edinburgh neither know nor care a great deal about Edinburgh's storied past. Of Mary Queen of Scots, John Knox, Randolph Murray, Montrose, Captain Porteous, Sir Walter Scott, and Professor Blackie, they reck not, and even Burke and Hare, the pioneer murderers, have been put out of mind by the exploits of more modern exponents of the fine art.

It is only when we have visitors that we remember there are such things as the Shrine and the Royal Observatory. It was a lady from London who first induced me to climb the Scott Monument. I had to have a Canadian show me how to use the Royal Scottish Museum. A Manxman who blew in from the South

African veldt hauled me out on my first circular tour of historic Edinburgh by charabanc, and later into nooks and crannies of the Castle which hitherto I had left to the spiders.

When you are turning from Princes Street into Leith Street, you will perceive at the base of Wellington's Statue to your left a monstrous multitude of citizens. You will find them standing there most of the day. Among them are some on business—for instance, street-bookmakers and pickpockets—but the majority are just standing there ; they cannot tell you why. Of this, however, you can be certain : they are not waiting for a chance to slip into Register House for the sake of browsing through their city's and their country's historic records. Similarly, there is no call to come early and avoid the crush at the National Library, at Lady Stair's House, at Huntly House, at the Outlook Tower, or at any other of Edinburgh's many historical, literary, and romantic peep-shows. All these places are well worth seeing, but they are not commonly the resort of the aborigines.

What the people of Edinburgh really revel in, is not the Edinburgh of antique glamour, but the chromium-plated Edinburgh of to-day. This may shock those who have acquired their preconceptions of the city from a reading of Scott's *Heart of Midlothian* or Stevenson's pleasant but already dated essay. The Heart of Midlothian is no longer the jailhouse of Sir Walter's great story, nor is it the heart-shape of cobble-stones which marks that romantic spot and on which the citizens spit in the passing for luck. The Heart of Midlothian now is a football team. If you do not believe me, ask to be directed to the Heart of Midlothian, and it will be a miracle if you are sent to Parliament Square and not to Tynecastle where the playing-field is.

To-day the citizens enjoy to the full the amenities of the city, its many green and open spaces—the Calton Hill, Arthur's Seat and the King's Park, Princes Street Gardens, and the like. They invade the Pentlands in their mobs on Sundays, not because Robert Louis Stevenson walked there once, but because they find these miniature Grampians a change from the town. They patronise all the city's modern pleasances, and have no attraction to the Pleasance of a previous age. They hie themselves to the splendidly laid out and richly stocked Zoo, the great open-air bathing pool at Portobello, and the extensive sea-front, now being recreated into one practically continuous promenade, from Cramond to Joppa.

Above all, Princes Street itself has captured their affections. They live there, one might say. This wide uninterrupted sweep from the shops on the North side to the Castle Rock on the South makes a street which must be adjudged great, however much they have monkeyed about with some of the minor details of scenery. It has stood up to many changes. You may point out that the architecture of the business side is a deplorable hotch-potch, hardly preferable æsthetically to the jumble of shooting galleries and ice-cream kiosks which make Portobello Front a town-planner's nightmare. Despite all this, Princes Street remains challengingly beautiful. It is the architectural inferior, one might argue, of George Street and Charlotte Square. But the one romantic pledge which your modern citizen of Edinburgh will permit himself is to die defending the fair name of Princes Street.

Do you wonder at this? Look with unjaundiced

eye, east, west, north, south ! East you will see Athens
perched on its hills. West, you will glimpse dazzling
towers and minarets, stalagmites of an enchanted cave.
North, from any corner, you will see the Firth of Forth
wrinkled with foam below you, and the distinct patch-
work of the fields and woods of Fife. South, you will
take in the impressive row of varied monuments, the
austere Greek art galleries on their terraced slope,
the luxuriant flowers and bushes, the trees, the soaring
grassland, the everlasting rock, and that rugged
serpentine sky-line from the Bridges to the West End,
with the thrawn crown of St Giles' and the jagged
crest of the Castle perfecting the suggestion of the craggy
humped back of some powerful dark dragon.

At your feet and at your elbow, all around you,
surges the living street itself, with its jostling humanity
of all classes, all kinds and colours, all ways of finding
salvation. To the majority of the people of Edinburgh
it has become a duty to walk on the shop side of Princes
Street. Ninety-nine per cent. of them, it seems, must
pass that way at least once a day or they are conscious
of the approach of death and disintegration. If you
are a lover of humanity, or a misanthrope, you cannot
find a better street in which to effervesce with enthusiasm
for the species, or be violently sick, for every known
variation of the stock of Adam and Eve decorates, or
infests, this famous boulevard, which the natives, by
the way, seldom call anything but " The Strand."
And few of them can tell you the road from there to
Sir Walter Scott's house, or how to get to the National
Portrait Gallery, or what statuettes are on the tiered
façade of Boots the Chemist's, or what Wellington on
his monument is doing with his hands.

The Princes Street parade has become an indispensable ritual of Edinburgh life. It goes on hour after hour from morn till midnight, day after day, year in, year out. Through the day it may have an ostensibly business purpose, but as night wears on and the places of business close their doors, you see it for what it is, a solemn ceremonial dedicated to the goddess whose street this is. Watch now how the faces liven up with interest in one another, how the eyes seek the passing eyes ! I have never reckoned out the chances of a fruitful or beneficial encounter, but the street inspires optimism and the seekers are loth to give up their quest.

Well, that is the kind of place the city really is, despite all rumours to the contrary. If you are a stranger you may be here to appreciate Edinburgh's wealth of associations, but you will soon find you have not come to the Egyptology section. Indeed, you will have to take good care that the place does not turn out to be too lively for your constitution.

If Princes Street is a mile for the worshippers of Venus, so you will find in Rose Street, which runs parallel with it, a mile for the Bacchanalians. And there are many other places where you are at liberty to go your royal mile. If you feel that in Rome you must do as the Romans, you will find that the zig-zag road along Rose Street is the primrose path which Scottish tradition favours, but it is only one of the many facile descents to Avernus in which the city abounds.

If pleasure be your quest, you will find here any number of dance halls and cafés dansants where the jazz is the same as where you come from, and even crazier. In the theatres you have a choice, as a rule, of London West End entertainment, London East End entertainment, or the native variety, which is by far the best of all. One of the few perceptible rudiments of a native culture in modern Scotland is the existence of a galaxy of distinguished Scots comedians, some of the best of whom are unknown in London and would not " take " there, as they are not " export " brands. If you explore too recklessly, you may find that the city indulges in leg-pulling, and that its air of respectability is really a screen for a gaiety almost Parisian. I know of no better city to make whoopee in than the city of John Knox, even though the reign of evil depicted in *Father Malachy's Miracle* is a thing of the past.

All the foregoing is by way of a warning. And here is another warning. Do not pay the slightest heed to the slander that the people of Edinburgh are frozen-faced and stuck-up, or that the city is really an exclusive club where the chances are you will be blackballed. Most of these stories come to you indirectly from Glasgow. Glasgow people say that when you call at a Glasgow house you are told, " Come in ! You're just in time for a cup o' tea " ; whereas in Edinburgh they say, " Come in ! You'll have had your tea ! " Glasgow people add that the people of Edinburgh are as cold as the east wind which perpetually blows through the streets of the Scottish capital. Don't believe it ! It is only to the people of Glasgow that the people of Edinburgh are so cold and unresponsive.

That east wind also is a myth. It is about as common in Edinburgh as the Aurora Borealis. The legend may be attributed to the patent fact that, when such a wind does come, you certainly get it in the neck in the principal streets of the city, which are laid east to west. But there are worse things than a good blow off the North Sea. Edinburgh is rather proud of that visitor from the east. The prevailing wind, the south-west, it ignores, since it seems to come from the neighbourhood of Glasgow. Nor is there so much rain in Edinburgh as that clever play about the city, " The Wind and the Rain," would have you believe. I could tell you a place where it rains a lot more, but the revelation might provoke a national crisis.

Take it from me, you will find Edinburgh a cosy place if you keep your coat on, and a city which, without shedding its antiquarian appeal, has provided itself with most of the modern conveniences. Make your sojourn here a protracted one, for the longer you are in the city the more you will like it. But if you are in a hurry, and must take in the sights in a day or two, here are some you must not miss :—

The Palace of Holyroodhouse, for its romantic Royal associations, ancient and modern ;

The Castle, of course, with emphasis on the Shrine, which is even more impressive and moving than you have been told ;

The Zoo, which is noted for its success in breeding animals and birds which do not naturally belong here, and which is as healthy for you as for its inmates, and a most delightful place to loaf about in ;

The Forth Bridge, especially on Sundays, when you have to look at bridges before you are legally entitled to a drink ;

The Corporation's magnificent open-air bathing-pool at Portobello ; also Portobello as an example of civic oversight ;

The Scott Monument, for the view ; and, if you want to see the city in five minutes,

The Camera Obscura in the Outlook Tower.

By the way, if you are genuinely interested in Edinburgh's history, the museum in the Outlook Tower, which is very near the Castle, tells you the whole story. Very few people in Edinburgh can tell you about the Outlook Tower, and I am pouting with pride as I offer this information.

In the years since the War, Edinburgh has lost something of its village appeal. Not so long ago, five minutes' stroll down Queensferry Street took one from Princes Street into cow-country. Now the housing schemes spread far and wide, and the country recedes into the distance. But there is a happy limit, for the sea and the hills cannot be pushed back, and so long as they do not build bungalows in Princes Street Gardens Edinburgh will remain a queen among cities.

by
J. R. ALLAN

Who would angle for the Leviathan
with a bent pin, or try to describe
Glasgow in three thousand words?
Not this writer, who does no more
than catch a few aspects of the city's
life

SKETCHES FOR A PORTRAIT OF GLASGOW

IT may seem presumptuous that I, an East Coaster, should dare to write about Glasgow, but I plead two things in extenuation.

To begin with, no native of Glasgow could write about his own town in less than three volumes, and even then he would be afraid that he had missed out just one more instance in which Glasgow is superior to all other cities of the earth together. Or, and such is the temper of these days, he would find life too short a time for setting down the miseries of life by the dirty waters of the Clyde. He would need a year to paint the smoke cloud that hangs so low upon the houses; another ten to describe the horror of mean grey streets; and a whole generation to examine the full wickedness of Glasgow bailies. The town breeds such an excess of love or hate in them that belong to it that I dare think there is a place for one who, being free from obligation to hate or love, can look upon the town with casual eyes.

But of course I am not casual about Glasgow; for, however lightly one may regard Heaven and Hell, Glasgow, that is part of both, cannot be turned off with a laugh. And thereby hangs my second plea. It is now eleven years since I first saw Glasgow through a February rain, and during that time I have been fascinated, repelled, enchanted, depressed with the town—but never bored. Sometimes when I worked in Glasgow I began to think that life was only an infinity of distant paydays, yet even at the worst moments, about the 20th of the month, the eternal good nature of the people made the lean days of waiting not only tolerable but amusing. Besides Glasgow, like the best cities, has some resources of free entertainment. The town and its people have a capacity for unexpectedness : you think you know all about them, then they surprise you with something new that is comic and terrible. Whatever else you may be, you are never bored ; and to be saved from boredom is one of the greater mercies in these days of too much entertainment. That is why I want to write about Glasgow. I can hardly say I love the town ; a million people and some thousand houses are too vast an object for a personal thing like love. But they have always made me curious and they have often rewarded my curiosity in unexpected ways. Therefore, out of gratitude, I would like to share some of that entertainment with you.

My introduction to Glasgow would have disposed anyone to favour the town. I was a student then and I had gone from Aberdeen to attend a conference of my own sort in the University at Gilmorehill. There was, I seem to remember, a certain amount of business intended to annoy the Senatuses of our Universities (a very proper object considering the ponderous nature of those bodies) ; but there were also, and these I remember clearly, many excellent lunches and dinners, the pleasantest kind of education for young men. We progressed in those studies, and afterwards small parties sat up late into the morning for the discussion of Life, with the help of gin and ginger ale.

61

It was after one of those sessions that we made to return to our hotel about three o'clock in the morning, a dozen young men all in excellent temper. Now that night had followed such a day as the people of Glasgow had not suffered for a generation. A great wind blew up on the wrath of God, tumbling down advertisement hoardings and chimney cans and roof slates in dreadful rain. These were not all. As if to make a sacrifice of vanities, the gale blew in the plate glass window of a ladies' drapery and carried many delicious garments over the town. Well, as we were making our way, lightly, through the West-end Park we discovered a garment abandoned by the wind on a thorn-bush near the statue of Thomas Carlyle. We took it down and thought of making it our emblem when someone had a better idea. He pointed to the statue and cried, " Old Tom's a-cold. Let's put him in the petticoat."

It was an excellent notion for three o'clock in the morning. We tucked the garment of rose-pink crêpe-de-chine under the beard of the grim philosopher where it hung coyly, or danced upon the night wind. As we stood there enraptured a policeman came along unseen and announced himself by a monitory cough. One or two of the politer spirits disappeared unobtrusively into the shadows, but the rest greeted the policeman hilariously, and before he had time to caution us, we had involved him in a kind of country dance in front of the statue. He was a very big and very solid policeman, but it may have been that the breezes in the West-end Park, music to so many amorous encounters, had been troubling his official wits with premonitions of the spring, for after some little hesitation he joined in the dance till the drops of sweat flew off his face like an April rain. At the end of the dance there was business with a mutchkin of gin, then we said good-night and went quietly home. Some little distance away I looked back and there was the policeman in the ring of light from the gas-lamp (that might have been an illuminated helmet) standing in front of the statue from which the delicate garment fluttered so gaily. There was about his back, I thought, the aspect of a man who has met with wonder in the night.

It is perhaps only in Glasgow that we would dare to be so frivolous or that the " polis " have still some little sense of wonder. A town like Glasgow is a great blessing to a small country like Scotland, for it is big enough to give you the relief of anonymity. It is almost impossible to be yourself in Scotland because, wherever you go, you are sure to be found out as somebody's relation, or employee, or friend ; and anything you do is likely to be told to that person with all the embroideries of triumphant malice. Thus it is very difficult ever to get away from your ordinary associations and be quite natural and foolish regardless of propriety, to do what you want instead of living up to your station in life. But Glasgow has infinite resources of refuge. If you fear discovery in the middle of the town you can go east into worlds that are unexplored by ordinary respectable Scotsmen and unmentionable by their wives. There, if you wish it, you can have freedom.

And, anywhere in Glasgow, you can have company. It is one of the glories of this town that the commoner citizens have a genius for casual friendship. In other parts of Scotland people are friendly enough once they know who you are, but they like to be sure of you before they commit themselves. The people of Glasgow

—with the exception of those who have sold themselves for a West-end accent—offer you friendship at sight. Undistinguished strangers have died of loneliness in the middle of an Edinburgh tea-party ; in Glasgow they would have been in danger of being overwhelmed with domesticity. Provided you have the power of listening sympathetically you need no other social accomplishment, for Glasgow people love few things better than telling you all about their families, their dogs, their football pools, their golf and their neighbours. Since they have hundreds of relations, thousands of friends and a million neighbours there is no danger that conversation will ever run dry. You can sink back on their friendly gossip like it was a feather-bed where you need have no fear of feeling the springs. They are a cosy people.

When I was a young man seeking diversion about the town we used to frequent the salon of a charming lady in one of the less distinguished quarters. Her house was composed of a room and kitchen, two stairs up. She and her husband, a silent man who could be eloquent about boilers, lived in the kitchen ; the room was sublet with board to a frisky little man who I understood was in the undertaking business. There was a large built-in bed in each room, but I don't know when the tenants slept in them because the house seemed full of visitors at any hour of the day and night.

You did not have to be invited ; somebody took you there for the first time ; afterwards you just went in. The scene was always much about the same. Our host sat in a broken-down easy-chair at one side of the fire, sucking an unlit pipe. Our hostess sat at the other side boiling a succession of kettles for tea. The lodger lay on the bed with his boots on a newspaper.

The visitors disposed themselves where they could. There was a great deal of conversation in the richest Glasgow dialect, each person contributing some personal observation on life. As these visitors worked at trades like sausage-making, paper-selling, betting, dancing in music halls and doorkeeping, they made some rare contributions to the sociology of Glasgow. For the most part all of us joined in the conversation, but if any had private matters to discuss, such as the raising of a temporary loan, they went through and sat on the lodger's bed, a liberty granted to all, provided they respected the bowler hat, his dearest possession. All the time our hostess boiled the kettles of water, the young ladies made tea, while those who happened to be flush contributed fish suppers and pies.

That, however, was not all. If, as occasionally happened, the ladies or gentlemen required something a little stronger, they bargained, quietly, with the lodger and, a deal having been made, he produced a pint from under the back of the bed. It was anonymous spirit, but it had a very definite effect and added to the friendliness of the party. The atmosphere of the room was warm and steamy on the raw winter nights; the visitors were wholly at ease; and to me that was the soul of Glasgow.

Of course that is not all Glasgow. Wherever there is great poverty there is usually great wealth, and Glasgow has many fine houses founded on the heartening Five Per Cents. Time was when anybody with a little capital could make a handsome competence in the town. Shipbuilding, shipowning, ironfounding, coal mining, importing, exporting, speculating—all these like horns of plenty showered their profits on Glasgow. The merchants transformed these profits into houses, collections of art, country estates and churches. Especially churches : either since their motto is " Let Glasgow flourish by the preaching of the Word " or, as an Englishman once said, because they thought the flood of wealth could be explained only by God having a corner in every counting-house.

The flood has subsided a little and many of the fine houses have become service flats ; but there are still plenty of rich people living on the meadows irrigated by that flood. I'm sorry that I can't tell you about the kind of life they enjoy ; but there are times when we suspect they are not quite the men their grandfathers were. There was a kind of Glasgow man who brought the town some honour. He bought pictures generously, if not always with discrimination ; he was ready to pay for music and even to listen to it ; he was sympathetic to all the arts. These men gave Glasgow an air, so that the ships coming up the Clyde brought not only canned meat and oranges but sometimes ideas of pleasure from the sophisticated world. Does that still happen? Who can say ? It is often difficult to know exactly what is happening round about us. But Glasgow does seem to lack the sort of figure—the man of fortune and vitality and enjoyment —she bred a generation ago. Sir Daniel Stevenson remains alone, a man of European interest, like a figure out of an heroic past, the friend of learning and music, the Patron of the democratic state. Maybe these times are not propitious when fortunes are hard to make and too uncertain when made. Besides, a Labour majority in the Town Council may have turned the minds of the well-to-do from culture to spiritual things, anticipating the imminent end of the world. But I remember I said that Glasgow is a town of the un-

expected. Who knows then what ideas may be ferment-
ing in Kelvinside and Pollokshields? Who knows?

But my mind always turns away from the drawing-
rooms to the streets of Glasgow for the sudden contrasts
that reveal so much of the town.

Once on a November afternoon I was walking along
Buchanan Street about half-past four o'clock. It was
a busy day : hundreds of fashionable women were
trafficking among the shops and the business men were
returning from or going to the coffee-rooms. There
was an atmosphere of money and well-being, the sort
of thing that makes you feel pleased with yourself as
long as you have a few shillings in your own pocket.
Then a procession came up the street, with blood-red
banners, that swayed menacingly under the misty
lights. These should have driven the women screaming
into the basements of the shops for they bore legends
in praise of Moscow, warnings about the wrath to
come. " Communists," the word flew along the pave-
ments. But no one screamed. The men that carried
the flags were broken beyond violence by the prolonged
misery of unemployment and could not sustain the
menace of the legends. The ladies in the fur coats
could look without fear on the procession, for it was
not the first stroke of revolt but another triumph of
law and order. A dozen constables were shepherding
the marchers, and they were such fine big men and
stepped along with such manly dignity that they
themselves were the procession. The unemployed
seemed to have no community with such defiant banners,
such splendid constables, and they may have known
it, for they walked without any spirit, as if they
realised they had no place in society, not even in their
demonstrations against it. The procession turned into

George Square. The unemployed dismissed and went home wearily to their bread and margarine. The constables eased their uniform pants and went off to the station with property and privilege resting securely on their broad shoulders. It was just another Glasgow afternoon.

Then some months later I was looking out from the window of a coffee-house in Argyle Street about seven o'clock of a Saturday evening. I heard fife music ; then a procession came out from St Enoch's Square. It was a company of Orangemen, or some such Protestants, in full uniform, back from an excursion in the country. They passed, an army terrible with banners, and comic, as men that have a good excuse for dressing up. They had just gone by when a new music came up to us and a new procession appeared, coming from Queen Street Station. They were Hibernians, or some other Catholic order, also returning from a day in the country ; terrible and comic also, after the fashion of their kind. Orangemen and Hibernians ! we said to ourselves. What will happen if they forgather ? Being wise youths and having some pleasure on hand, we did not follow to see. But we met a man some time later that night who swore he had been present. The Hibernians, he said, discovered that the Orangemen were in front, so they quickened their pace. The Orangemen, hearing also, slackened theirs. Some resourceful and sporting policemen diverted both parties into a side street and left them to fight it out. After half an hour, when all the fighters had thoroughly disorganised each other, bodies of police arrived, sorted the wounded from the winded and despatched them to their proper destinations in ambulances and plain vans. That is the story as it was told to me and I cannot swear that it is true in every detail; but it might have happened in Glasgow that way, and I doubt if it could have happened in any other town. Such incidents give Glasgow afternoons and evenings their distinctive flavour.

This is not a critical essay on Glasgow, but an attempt to give you some impressions of life as I have seen it there; so I will conclude the matter with the case of the Admiral and his wooden leg.

Now the Admiral is, I think, very typical of thousands of people who live in Glasgow. He is not a native of the town: he belongs to the north and he has come south in search of his fortune. Nor is he an Admiral; but he followed the sea in his youth and he retains something of the amplitude of the great waters which has won him the affectionate by-name. He is a man of presence, of ingenuity, of humour: a Glasgow character, or to be more precise, one of those who give character to Glasgow. And he has an artificial leg, of which all his friends are somehow proud.

Now it has often been our pleasure to go in a company and play golf on one of the courses to the south of Glasgow. You might think that the artificial leg would be a disadvantage in the game; but no, the Admiral swears that it is the foundation of his excellence, as it provides him with an immobile pivot upon which he can swing with the exactitude so desirable in golf. Perhaps he is right, for he can play as well with his one native leg as the rest of us can play with two. At any rate you will understand that he is a man of considerable resource, and that is the point of the story.

We were playing a match at Eaglesham, up on the windy Renfrewshire moors, the Admiral and I against two others of our company. The rigidity of the leg, coupled with some luck on my part, gave us a slight advantage, so that we were one hole up with two to play. Our opponents, however, did not consider themselves beaten ; and, as five shillings depended on the match, they were making a great effort to win. It was then that the accident happened. After playing a very excellent recovery shot out of some long grass into which I had foolishly driven our ball, the Admiral staggered and fell on the ground, crying, " Hold on, lads, I'm wounded." It was a cry fit to be remembered among the last words of great commanders ; but on this occasion there were no tearful scenes in the cockpit. " I've broken my leg," the Admiral said ; and we were dismayed, for it is not usual to find spare legs upon a golf course. " But I'll soon mend it," he added. He pulled up his trouser, unlimbered the leg, and inspected the damage. We waited his decision anxiously. " Five minutes," he said. Then he took a repair outfit from his poacher's pocket—a pliers, some wire, bits of leather, nuts, bolts, screws and twine ; and there, on the spot where he had fallen, did an excellent bit of surgery, with fingers skilled in repairing small mischances. Four and a half minutes later he stood erect again and proceeded to win the match with a masterly shot out of a bunker. Surely Glasgow will always flourish as long as she can attract men with spirit and resource like his.

There are many other things that should be drawn into a portrait of Glasgow. The coffee-rooms, for instance, where the business men gather for refreshment and gossip after a hard hour's work in their offices. They are not impressive, for the clothes and the fashions of this age have no dignity. The neat dark suit and the respectable bowler hat do not give a man a chance and those who wear them diminish in stature. After spending half an hour in a Glasgow coffee-room you begin to wish for the massive heads, the curling lapels and the patriarchal whiskers of Victorian days. And you also begin to wonder how the alleged rush and bustle of commerce allows so much time for coffee and discussion. But perhaps the gentlemen are planning, planning, ceaselessly and for ever planning. There are also the tea shops where the ladies refresh themselves after an hour of shopping. The consumption of cream buns is enormous ; eclairs die in thousands ; chocolate biscuits melt away as in thaw. It is perhaps not a wonderful thing that there are so many comfortable ladies in Glasgow when they do themselves so well in the afternoon. And there are the excursions down to the Coast. It is good entertainment to go to Largs on a Saturday afternoon in summer and watch the citizens at play ; it is an unforgettable experience to return with the last train and travel seventeen in a carriage. You can't be stand-offish then. You have got to be a mixer. Gentlemen offer you warm beer out of screw-top bottles ; stout ladies hand round sweets in sticky papers ; babies crawl over you, leaving thumb-prints on your face. There is singing, not sweet but hearty. There is a total lack of fresh air. You are for the moment one of the great mass of humanity and you simply can't deny it. There are a lot of East Coast people who ought to ride in the last train home from Largs.

Does any idea of the town emerge from these impressions ? Perhaps they are not enough related to each other. Yet I do think they have something in common that comes near to the quality of Glasgow. The town is dreadful in many ways. It is ugly in itself, and too many people must live in a way that denies expression to the best qualities within them. But the life of the people has a richness, a warmth and a humour such as you do not find in any other part of Scotland and which, if it were allowed a free expression, might transform Glasgow into a very wonderful town. Unfortunately other people have discovered those qualities, accept them complacently, and think they justify all that is bad. Perhaps that complacency will be destroyed some day, for ever. Then Heaven knows what wonderful things may come out of Glasgow.

BREAD AND BUTTER

by
C. A. OAKLEY

Glasgow is not the only manufacturing
town in Scotland. The Director of
the Scottish Division of the National
Institute of Industrial Psychology
makes a short survey here of the
variety and diffusion of our trades

TOWNS AND TRADES

AN unusually large number of people in Scotland work for their livings. They do hard manual work forty-eight hours every week, and they do it very well. Indeed, the Scot, undistinguished though he is in some respects, may be claimed, with considerable justification, to be the best " skilled " worker in the world. Undoubtedly the imprint *Scottish-made* is regarded everywhere as a mark of quality.

There were, of course, not many industries anywhere before the middle of the eighteenth century—although some European factories were employing as many as a thousand workers as far back as medieval times— but Scotland had even fewer than the few in other countries. Communities of spinners and weavers did grow up in the eastern Borders, in Fife, and in the Aberdeen district ; and there were able craftsmen in Edinburgh. But their numbers were not many and it can be said without much exaggeration that up to two hundred years ago there was really no industry at all comparable to modern Scottish industry.

Even to-day Scotland as a whole is not really industrialised. But a part of it is highly industrialised. This part runs as a diagonal belt, about forty miles broad, across Scotland. The southern boundary starts at Ayr and ends in the Firth of Forth. It is drawn just south of Edinburgh so as to include a coal-mining district which has Dalkeith and Tranent as its chief towns. The northern boundary is a line joining Dumbarton and Montrose. Almost everyone in Scotland—not far short of 90 per cent. of the population —lives within this narrow belt, and the most important exception—Aberdeen—is not so many miles north of Montrose.

Outside of the industrial belt the number of inhabitants per acre is very small, and the people are engaged in work which may be described as traditional —that is to say, farming, making woollen and linen textiles, and catching herring. One of the chief products of these parts is poets and, for one hundred and fifty years, they have spent more than a little of their time saying unpleasant things about Glasgow's smoky chimney stalks. During the early 'thirties, however, these stalks stopped being smoky, and then they waxed indignant about that. But the recovery has come, and with it Glasgow is once again hearing itself described as a (or alternatively *the*) blot on the fair face of Scotland.

It is, truly enough, hard to realise that, only two hundred years ago, Glasgow was a pleasant little ecclesiastical town, situated beside a salmon river, and much praised by visitors for its beauty. Its destiny was changed by the Act of Union with England, which opened up legitimate commerce between Scotland and the American (including the West Indian) Colonies. Previously Scotland's chief ports—Aberdeen and Leith —had been east-coast ports ; but the new trade called for a west-coast port, and, after a century of grim rivalry between Glasgow and Greenock, Glasgow won the position of being Scotland's greatest port.

Several young Glasgow merchants two hundred years ago displayed great enterprise, and their names have been perpetuated in the streets west of Glasgow Cross, such as Glassford Street, in which they did their business. Their concern was chiefly with tobacco and sugar. They began by bartering Scottish manufactured goods and foodstuffs for the products of the plantations, and thus many manufacturing industries and the shipping industry were developed as a result of this new trade. During the decades which followed, the Tobacco Lords, as they were called, rose to great prominence. Glasgow has still many tales to tell of the arrogance with which they flaunted their flowing red robes before the populace, as they made their way to the Tontine Hotel. It should also be remembered, however, that they captured more than half of the English tobacco merchants' business and so began the process of raising Scotland from the squalor of poverty. No longer had Scotsmen to cringe for English " siller." Now they could make silver for themselves.

But great disaster was to befall these merchants, for with the American War of Independence they lost, not only their business, but also the money which they had lent to the American planters. It was the first of several acute crises which the industries of the Glasgow district were to undergo during these two hundred years. Yet they have emerged from each crisis stronger than ever before.

" Glasgow men never know when they are beaten," say the Glasgow men, adapting Napoleon to suit themselves. " Glasgow men have the de'il's own luck," say the Edinburgh men as a variation of their usual criticisms. And the onlooker can say that both are right. For instance, the Glasgow men were fortunate in that just when they were looking for a new business to take the place of their tobacco trade, Arkwright, Compton and others were revolutionising textile processes and opening the way for the cotton industry. On the other hand, it must be recognised that the Glasgow men *did* have the intelligence and the enterprise to recognise at a very early stage the significance of these changes.

For the next sixty years the Glasgow district was the most important centre of the world's cotton industry. Then it had to meet another tremendous crisis, which was again brought about by an American war—this time, the Civil War. It might be worth while at this point, incidentally, to remind American readers that the subject of American and British debts is more complex than their politicians may have led them to suppose.

It is not easy for us to appreciate the reasons which caused Glasgow to throw away so much of its cotton industry at that time. After all, Lancashire was hit too, yet it emerged from the troublous times not only in a healthier state than ever, but with much of Glasgow's industry as well. To-day, comparatively little is left of the once famous West of Scotland cotton industry, except for the great Paisley thread mills, and some branches at the high quality end of the trade, associated particularly with shirtings, furnishings, muslin and lace.

Why should this have happened? Well, it would seem that the Glasgow cotton textile manufacturer was much exasperated by the way in which American internal quarrels had upset his business ; and, while he was in this frame of mind, the heavy industries, based upon coal and iron, began to make big profits. The Blackband seam of iron-ore, in the Coatbridge district, had been discovered (and was being worked to death), and, turning his eyes to this new field, the Glasgow man's attitude to his capricious cotton industry was " Ach, t' hell " ; and, after he had extracted every possible penny from his mills and factories, he just allowed them to die. He couldn't be bothered with them. But if he had not been quite so lacking in imagination, how big, I wonder, would Glasgow be to-day ? For, against this rather sordid story must be placed the fact that the Glasgow man really has made a great success of these heavy industries.

They continued to expand for several decades — until the 1921 period—and they raised Glasgow to the position of Second City of the British Empire. Even at the present time when Glasgow, according to population figures, is only the Sixth City, it must be realised that the population of Greater Glasgow, if calculated in the same way as that of Greater London, is two millions.

The Glasgow district nowadays makes almost everything. Its products must certainly be the most varied in the British Empire, perhaps in the world. It is the chief centre in the Empire for such different articles as the finest ships, boilers, carpets, knitted outerwear, peak caps, thread, wringers, sewing machines, and clay tobacco pipes ! One of its firms had no fewer than 42,000 employees in 1918.

Perhaps the chief influence in bringing about this remarkable development has been shipbuilding. Ships are self-contained vessels and they must be supplied with everything that a modern hotel is supplied with. So there has been a great inducement for the establishment of factories on Clydeside to make such a variety of articles as furniture, kitchen equipment, sanitary appliances, and air-conditioning apparatus.

Accordingly, the collapse of the world's shipping industry during the depression was a complete disaster to the Glasgow district. Not only did it cry halt to shipbuilding but to all of these ancillary industries as well. Now there has been a grand recovery, but the people of Glasgow do not need to be told that it is in no small part attributable to rearmament. World trade is still in an unhealthy state and comparatively few new merchant ships are being constructed.

Yet Glasgow *is* going to emerge from this crisis greater than ever. Why? Well, partly because of its security from air attack by hostile countries. Many firms whose factories are in the London-Birmingham belt have become very conscious of the disadvantages of having all their eggs in one basket. Several are also having difficulty because of an inadequate supply of skilled labour, and they realise that there is an immense source to draw on in the Glasgow district. They have, therefore, good reasons for setting up branch factories on Clydeside and, in fact, for transferring their main works to Clydeside.

*   *   *   *

The industries of the other parts of Scotland rarely get a fair show in a chapter such as this. Editors quite naturally turn to Glasgow men to write about Scottish industries. But usually they just write about the industries of the West of Scotland and conclude with a paragraph or two in which they make passing reference, perhaps, to the Border tweed industry (without perhaps realising that there is a northern tweed district as well as a southern tweed district), to the Dunfermline linen industry (but why always Dunfermline, when there are more linen works in Kirkcaldy than in Dunfermline, and the industry besides being distributed throughout Fife and Angus, extends as far north as Aberdeen ?), to the Dundee jute industry, and to the fishing (without making the vitally important distinction between white fish and herring). Frequently they take no notice at all of Edinburgh.

No Scottish industrial town receives so little recognition as Edinburgh, although the fault begins with Edinburgh itself, for it scarcely deigns to recognise its chief industrial district, Leith. Delicate nostrils in Princes Street are turned towards the Castle lest a north wind should outrage them with odours of whisky, tallow, oil, vinegar, or even—perish the thought !—cured fish. Yet some of us think that the most interesting pennyworth in the tram from the Post Office is down Leith Walk and not along Princes Street.

There are some facts about the Edinburgh district which everybody in Scotland ought to know (and very few do know). It is the centre of British fine-printing industry ; it is one of the chief paper-making districts in Great Britain ; it is the second largest brewing district in Great Britain (a fact which prompted the Editor of this book to make his home for a time in Edinburgh) ; it is one of the largest biscuit manu-facturing districts ; and its great firms include the second largest British firm in the rubber industry, the largest electrical engineering firm in Scotland, and one of the best-known British structural engineering firms. There are many others who, although they are not such large employers of labour, are quite important. Such firms are the chief Scottish manufacturers of oatmeal, cut-glass, printing ink, and paper-making machinery. The truth of the matter is that most of Auld Reekie's smoke comes from factory stalks and not from advocates' fire-places, school boiler-houses, and novelists' pipes.

*   *   *   *

There are no large towns in the Borders, but industrially the district is well-known throughout the world, chiefly because of its tweeds. The tweed industry has, however, been cruelly treated by foreign tariffs, quotas, and embargos. The world demand for these hard - wearing, brightly - patterned materials is un-doubtedly greater than ever. But the potential customers cannot buy and, what is worse, sometimes cannot pay for what they have bought.

Tweeds are woven in other districts besides Galashiels, Hawick, Selkirk, and Peebles. There are large works in Edinburgh and Aberdeen. A belt of small towns engaged in the industry spreads from Aberdeen to Inverness, and there is also the hand-weaving industry of the Highlands and of the Islands, best known to the world through its Harris tweeds.

Alongside the tweed industry there has grown up the hosiery industry. It has made relatively the greater progress in recent years. Many scores of factories are knitting underwear and outerwear, in woollen, rayon, cotton and other yarns. The quality of the Scottish products is very high. Factories have been established in almost all parts of Scotland ranging from Annan by the Solway Firth to Huntly in Aberdeen-shire. A famous section of the industry comprises the hand-knitting done in so many homes in Shetland. The most successful branch of the woollen textile industry since the War has been carpet-making. It has benefited both from the housing boom and from improvement in public taste. The largest firm have several works in Glasgow and their extensions have been the most impressive in Glasgow during the last decade. Another firm who have increased their business very considerably are located in Kilmarnock. Other large factories are situated in Ayr, Elderslie, Paisley, and Glasgow.

Textiles play a large part in the industrial life of Scotland. The town of Dundee—second in importance only to Glasgow—has been created around the jute industry. The almost complete centralisation of this industry in a single district is one of the most remarkable features of British industrial organisation.

Only within the last hundred years have the commercial possibilities of jute been appreciated. The fibre comes from India and is cheap. Accordingly, jute cloth is very suitable for making into bags and packing material. But the industry has created a serious rival for itself. During recent decades, Dundee merchants have been establishing works in Calcutta ; and Dundee textile engineers have supplied them with their machinery. Now the production of the Indian mills and factories is five times as great as Dundee's. And so the Dundee spinner and the Dundee weaver are fighting Asiatic competition *coming from within the Empire*. The Government is fully alive to the seriousness of the position, but it is a terribly difficult problem to deal with.

Besides the woollen industry, the traditional Scottish textile industry is the linen industry ; and, just as the former was located in the districts best supplied with raw material—that is to say, the best sheep—so the latter was located in the agricultural district most suitable for the cultivation of flax. That district is East Central Scotland—Fife and its neighbouring counties. Dunfermline became the centre of the finer branches of the industry, the weights growing progressively heavier the farther the situation of the factories from Dunfermline.

Since the War, and particularly since 1930, the fine linen industry has had a bad time. The public demand for fine linen fabrics has fallen off—partly due to encroachment by cotton fabrics. Keen competition has been experienced from Northern Ireland, where rates of wages are said to be rather less than in Scotland, and the American market, formerly the great market for Scottish linens, almost disappeared during the depression.

A new industry (or rather an old industry restored) has taken its place. Tariffs have made it cheaper to weave natural silk fabrics in this country than in Switzerland and Austria. Several new firms in Dunfermline are engaged in this work, the excellence and availability of highly-skilled weavers being largely responsible for this development. It has also kept the town's embroidery works busy. The heavier linens of the canvas type were not affected by the slump so badly and, as they are used for many purposes by the fighting forces, the rearmament programme has kept most of the mills and factories busy.

One branch of the textile industry which was fully occupied throughout the depression was the making of linoleums. To-day this is Kirkcaldy's great industry and provides one of those interesting cases of an industry which has been moving north in recent years. The town is well known in Scotland to-day for its characteristic smell of linseed oil.

Several other branches of Scottish textile industry can be only mentioned in this chapter—for instance, artificial silk is being prepared in a large works recently built at Jedburgh, the silk throwsters of Motherwell and Govan are busy, ropes and fishing-nets are being made by several firms, and there have been several extensions of the Glasgow garment-making industry.

*　　*　　*　　*

In spite of the size and variety of the textile industry in the Scottish industrial belt, it is not the chief industry of the district. This is coal and iron. There are five major sections of the coal-field. The Lanarkshire section is showing signs of exhaustion and there has been a tendency for the industry to drift back to the East Coast, where it had its origin several centuries ago. The chief developments of the present day are going on in Fife and in the Lothians. Drilling for oil is now being carried out in the Dalkeith district and, while it would be foolish to be optimistic, the choice may be considered more promising than most of the others in which experiments have been made. It should perhaps be pointed out that, although the shale-oil industry began in the Lothians, there is no connection between the presence of oil-bearing shale and the present drilling. Shale is mined in much the same way as coal is mined.

The oldest centre of the iron industry is Coatbridge, a town famous for its pig-iron and for its tubes. The more modern steel industry has Motherwell as its focus. The Scottish steel industry has been rationalised during the last few years and is, at the present time, fully occupied. The iron industry has tended to lag behind, but the last two years have brought back much prosperity to the Coatbridge district and recent announcements of factory extensions have restored confidence.

The busiest section of the industry has been iron-founding at Falkirk. It is particularly associated with the manufacture of baths, cookers, rain-water goods, and other appliances which have been in considerable demand recently owing to the housing boom.

*   *   *   *

Aberdeen, the only large town outside of the industrial belt, has many industries. It is the third of the British white-fish ports. It supplies Great Britain with much of its granite. It has five large paper-mills. It has large woollen and linen works. And it has several medium-sized engineering firms who send their products to all parts of the world.

The food-canning industry had its origin in Aberdeen. During recent years this industry has extended in a remarkable way, largely because of the invention of better methods of exhausting the air and vapours from the tins. Fish is now being canned in Aberdeen, Peterhead, Fraserburgh and Dundee. Fruit is being canned in Montrose, Dundee, Carluke and other towns.

*   *   *   *

The district north and west of Aberdeen comprises more than half of Scotland—at least, in area. It is sparsely populated. Others are dealing in this book with the industrial problems of the Highlands and the Islands, so they will be merely mentioned here. Actually there are two distinct problems. The people who live in the ports around the north-east coast, and who are incidentally of Norse not Celtic stock, are chiefly engaged in the herring industry. It is experiencing calamitous times, for its continental markets have dwindled, partly due to the financial policy of certain foreign countries, but partly due to the fact that these countries have built high-powered trawlers and are doing their own fishing.

There are few other industries in the north—except of course, the woollen textile industry. The most important are engineering—there are large works at Fraserburgh and Inverness — and the aluminium industry at Fort William. As I write there are reasonably good hopes that, Inverness notwithstanding, Fort William will get some, although no longer the whole, of the new carbide industry.

*　　*　　*　　*

The mention of Aberdeen and of the North-East counties immediately brings to mind — agriculture. And agriculture brings to mind—foodstuffs. When a farmer thinks of foodstuffs he thinks of natural food-stuffs, closely related to the soil. But when an industrialist thinks of food-stuffs he thinks of manu-factured food-stuffs. This chapter is being written from his standpoint, and in what better way could it end than with a suggestion of " stomach-appeal " ? Scotland has a great reputation for making things to eat. Is she not known as the Land o' Cakes ?

The link between natural and manufactured food-stuffs is to be found in such comestibles as oatmeal, jam, and, needless to say, haggis. Although nothing like as much oatmeal is consumed by the average individual as formerly, it must be remembered that the number of individuals has increased, for there are a great many more people in Great Britain than there used to be. Accordingly, there are several factories— some of them model factories—actively engaged in making oatmeal and in doing it up in modern packets. Jam and marmalade are made by several firms in Dundee and, in the Glasgow district, at Paisley, Carluke, Baillieston and elsewhere. Most of these preserves are of very high quality.

The displays of cakes and scones in Scottish bakers' windows make the mouth water. One has to come to Scotland in order to taste most of the perishable delicacies, although things like shortbread and Dundee cake are sold throughout Great Britain. Out of the baking industry has come the biscuit industry, and since the War it has grown to be of considerable size. There are many large biscuit factories in Edinburgh and Glasgow, and almost without exception they have had to extend their works within the last few years.

Another notable Scottish industry is sweet-making. The outstanding development here has been the extension of the retail manufacturers' businesses. Their shops have penetrated far into England. Two of the firms have over two hundred shops and a third is approaching its first hundred.

Several famous proprietary food-stuffs are made in Scotland. They include coffee essence, corn-flour, semolina and custard-powder. No one would challenge the claim that the chemists' departments of some firms have displayed great ingenuity in recent years.

It is odd to think that, in this land with so many things to eat, living only two hundred years ago was amongst the most frugal to be found in any European country. And it might still be, but for the fact that Scottish industry has grown up in the meantime.

by
IAN MACPHERSON

The Scottish country tradesman has been an important and diverting figure for generations. His chances of survival in this highly organised world are discussed in the following pages

COUNTRY TRADES

SMALL country industries serve a double purpose within a nation. They preserve the countryside as a thing distinct from the town, having its own self-centred life. If there were no country industries serving agriculture or making use of the products of the farm, then the country would degenerate until it was simply a factory feeding the cities ; and the cities, selling farmers their implements, their clothes, their dishes—everything the farmer used, from ploughs to platters—then buying all the farmers produced, would shortly control the country wholly.

But small country industries also help to keep individual taste alive in a mass-producing world where men must perforce standardise their likings to keep the conveyor belts moving. The country industry, being small, is not the slave of its own efficient machinery ; it can change its plans, alter its designs, without spending tens of thousands of pounds and throwing men out of work while the changes take place ; being in the country it is out of the shadow of the huge firms and escapes the inferiority complex which makes small town industries try to imitate their powerful rivals—until they imitate themselves to death.

Perhaps country industries have a third virtue, though it was more marked last century than it is now.

They are able to experiment with new designs, new processes, which are often copied by their city rivals. They give their employees an all-round training and there are small engineering firms in the country which cannot retain their workmen because they are snapped up by large firms who, employing machine-minders, cannot by any chance produce engineers.

Scotland fortunately still possesses a great variety of country industries. Two of these require no introduction. Their products, Scotch whisky and Scottish woollens, are world-famous.

The real Scotch whisky—that is, malt whisky produced by the fermentation of barley in peaty water—is, of course, entirely a product of the Scottish country. There are distilleries in our cities "making" grain whisky but that is not Scotch whisky. It is a spirit which can be produced anywhere in the world and is used as occasion arises to blend with malt whisky for the undiscriminating palates of to-day, and especially of England to-day—or to make methylated spirits and other commercial spirits. But Scotch whisky is *malt* whisky. There is nothing in the world like it. It requires and repays a cultivated taste. It is made in the Highlands. And since prohibition was repealed America has taken so much of it that Scottish distilleries are busier than they have been for many years. One ought not to visit Scotland without tasting her malt whisky. It may not be too easy to get. English customs are debasing our tastes and even good Scotsmen now drink blends of grain and malt whisky. You are more likely to get it in a " pub " than in a hotel.

Scottish woollens share the world-repute of Scotch whisky. They are made in comparatively small factories and mills, and in the country—for the famous Border wool-manufacturing towns, Selkirk, Galashiels, Hawick, are small towns and essentially country towns. They do not compete with Yorkshire. They make tweeds of high quality in medium-sized mills. They have, alas, suffered sadly because of the quota system for exports. Tariffs could not keep their cloths out of the countries to which they used to be exported because people abroad were prepared to pay highly for them. But the quota system takes no account of what people want in the country where it is applied.

The Borders produce more woollens than any other part of Scotland. It was not so always. "Galloway for 'oo'" is an old saying, but Galloway nowadays has very few wool-mills. Those that it still keeps are quite small and are therefore prosperous, one or two of them being so busy that they cannot cope with the work they get. They are more successful to-day than the Border mills because they are small enough to be superintended by their owners ; they can develop new styles, new designs, switch from tweeds for suits to rugs for cars, make scarves, blankets, gay shawls, and lead fashion instead of following it. One may find the produce of these mills in all the high-class shops in Britain, and in America too. Any man who has time to spare for a visit to Galloway should not leave Newton-Stewart without visiting its wool-mills ; one manufactures on power and hand-looms both, the other entirely on hand-looms.

Scarcely a Scottish county lacks its wool-mills. In some cases they use locally-grown wool and produce cloth for a local demand. But wherever the miller is a man of taste and enterprise the scope of his business has extended and townsfolk seek him out. Sometimes we grow weary of the tyranny of cheapness in standard colours. The Highlands have of course their woollens too.

The Hebrides produce their famous Harris tweed, hand-woven in the crofters' own homes and dyed with the traditional vegetable dyes prepared from such homely things as moss and onion skins. The value of the trade in Harris tweed has increased enormously since it was protected from unscrupulous imitators (including, of course, both Scotsmen and the egregious Japanese) by a Board of Trade mark. Harris tweed goes in bales to America now where the best standard-isers in the world will pay sweetly for novelties from abroad.

One must not forget Shetland with its lovely soft knitted wear, its scarves so fine they are like silk, its stockings, its gloves and Fair Isle jumpers with their traditional designs. Shetland wool is not clipped from the sheep but plucked away, or " rou'ed " when it is ripe to fall off and this has a great deal to do with its softness.

The manufacture of furniture has passed from the hands of the country joiners and cabinet-makers in Scotland who used to make those solid dressers for farm kitchens, those huge mahogany sideboards, for which our modern rooms have no space and our hasty modern minds little desire ; they last too long. But the making of furniture in Scotland still keeps to the verge of the country. Towns of moderate size, like Beith in Ayrshire, fashion our smaller chairs and tables, our flimsier wardrobes and chests of drawers.

The way in which such a standardised and mass-producing industry as the manufacture of furniture has in Scotland clung to the small country towns where it was once practised on a small scale is typically Scottish, and one difficulty in speaking about Scottish country industries is to define them, for there are industries in our little towns, and even in the depths of the country, which differ from city industries only in their location. For instance the lace-mills in Ayrshire are situated in small villages in a very pretty, very rural glen above Kilmarnock. Is the manufacture of lace therefore a country industry? I think one must say yes; it does not differ in kind from lace-making in a city but it does differ in size. Our Ayrshire lace-mills are small, they have grown into the life of the villages where they are situated. To hear the women in these mills singing Scots songs at their work, and to see the village windows proud with lace curtains, is to be persuaded that a mill in the country, though it makes the same things as its city rivals, has its peculiar character and own virtues. Even the cotton-mill in the village of Sorn is less grim than cotton-mills in large towns. The country scene sometimes redeems industrialisation.

Of course Scotland is a country with four cities, only one of them being really large as modern cities go; it has several fairly large towns, but for the rest its towns are small, and many places that we call towns would be villages in England. Our industries, therefore, if they exist outside the four cities must come pretty near to being in the country. They find themselves in country towns or villages, as brewing does in Alloa. Scottish agricultural implement makers do not migrate to the cities, nor do they grow so large that cities gather round them as is the case in England and America. But our implement makers pursue their trade in little towns like Huntly, Alloa, and Maybole. Linen is made in towns of moderate size in Scotland, and of course wool-milling is still a country industry.

But besides those industries which place themselves in the country or the town indifferently, and would manufacture the same things in Glasgow or Ecclefechan, there are many small industries which are entirely of the country. They remain in the rural parts of Scotland for one of three reasons : they are dependent on local resources, or local markets, or they are traditionally tied to the place where they were established long ago.

The country industries which depend on local resources, or serve a local market, have their parallels in every nation. Those that exploit country resources are quarries, brickworks, lime-kilns, bobbin-mills, saw-mills—and in a wider sense distilleries and creameries which use a *cultivated* local resource. These country industries depend on the export of their manufactures. The granite of Aberdeen and Kirkcudbright, the slate of Ballachulish, the whisky of the north, and the butter and cheese and condensed milk of the south-west, must be sold to a wider market than the country round provides. Even our lime-kilns look for a national market for their lime ; the bobbin-mills sell their bobbins to the Yorkshire wool-manufacturers and the cotton manufacturers of Lancashire. Perhaps one must nowadays exempt brickworks from the category of country industries which export their products. They did so until recently, but when the country parts of Scotland took to building new houses, and fabricated them of brick instead of the traditional but dearer stone, then the small Scottish brickworks found that they could scarcely supply the local demand for bricks.

Rural industries of a differing sort are those which supply a local demand, as do the vanishing cartwrights ; or the blacksmiths who make ploughs and other simple agricultural implements specially designed for local use. But even these, when they attain a certain success locally, begin to look afield, and it is out of them that the large agricultural engineering firms, and some firms of general engineering, ultimately grow. Industry owes an enormous debt to the small men of the countryside, the joiners and smiths. The bicycle came first from a Dumfriesshire smiddy; the steamship originated in the tiny shop of a Dumfriesshire engineer; nearly all our modern farm implements had their origin in the skill and brains of country tradesmen whose descendents these implements are now robbing of their work.

But lastly, and in a sense most truly of the country, come industries which are traditional in rural Scotland and would not if they could alter their habitat. Scotland has many linen-mills but only one hand-loom weaver of linen, who resides in Laurencekirk as did his forebears for centuries. His business still thrives and employs labour in spite of the competition of the machine. He has a tradition behind him which aids him doubly; his firm is known and its work respected. And he himself, conscious of the force of the tradition behind him, stays content with a quiet business of modest size producing fine work. Modernity which rages so violently against the things our forebears respected, taste and individual skill, pits itself in his case not against one man, its own child, but against an inherited attitude.

One may find the same thing exemplified in a very different business in Sanquhar in Dumfriesshire where there is a firm of farm and forest tool-makers established since almost two hundred years. It has been famous all these years for the quality of its tools; its name is respected; and therefore it cannot, even if it would, deny its traditions. If a new firm were to arise, making similar tools to those that are made in Sanquhar, its tendency would be to imitate the Sheffield forgers who turn out picks so cheaply that they are not worth resharping when they are blunted ; it is cheaper to buy a new head. It is difficult, almost impossible, for a new firm to establish itself to-day by producing things of high quality, and therefore we are dependent for a good deal of which we would be impoverished if we lost, to the businesses which live on a tradition of fine workmanship.

In the eighteenth century, Scotland's grim but still golden age, the snuff-boxes of Mauchline were famous. Famous painters painted miniatures on them, and some boxes were sold for hundreds of pounds. Their chief distinguishing feature was their wooden hinges, so exquisitely made they are to this day as free and firm as when they were new out of Ayrshire. The firm in Mauchline now makes cheap whitewood boxes and enjoys, strangely enough, some respect because of its romantic history, even though the things it makes now are far from the same as the snuff-boxes which earned it fame.

Tradition plus common-sense is at sufficient variance with modern ideas and fashions in Dumfriesshire to keep clog-makers fairly busy in that county still. Scotland's best basket-makers are the tinkers, and one could scarcely give the name of industry to anything that occupied their idle hands. But there is a small and not very important basket-making industry in Skye where the crofters' hands, as idle and less skilled than the tinkers', weave shopping baskets in their too-plentiful leisure. We had once a great many country potteries which made crocks of the plainest sort for farm and cottar-house kitchens, but they are dead. But a new pottery has been established in Kirkcudbright. In England there are many prosperous little potteries making cheap pretty dishes. Then here and there through the country one may find strange little industries ; a firm in Renfrewshire makes blocks by hand for printing flags—the world's militant mood should help this trade. And Renfrewshire has also the famous hand-weavers of tartan at Kilbarchan. A little foundry in Langholm makes fire-savers for the enormous kitchen ranges of Eskdale and Cumberland. Tinsmiths in the dairying counties try to convince farmers that good milk-pails and basins are cheap in the long run.

In Scotland there are fewer country industries than there were. But such as remain keep a tradition of good workmanship alive in an age when the shoddy is in the ascendant. Some men say that they are doomed, and the city will take everything at last. A gallant fight is never in vain. If we lose them we shall lose variety and individual enterprise. But they have survived storms as bad as that which blows at present. We may not always continue to live for to-day, nor to prefer towns and cities to country life.

by
J. R. ALLAN

Agriculture is still our greatest producing industry ; and this article shows
how a very important part of the
nation have adapted themselves to
changing conditions during the last
fifteen years

THE FARMER AND THE FUTURE

AGRICULTURE, in common with all other Scottish industries, except the manufacture of cheap food and cheaper amusement, has suffered (and changed) since 1921. It may have suffered rather less than its leaders would have made the Government and the public believe, since a farmer in pursuit of pity has never hidden his woes under his own bushel : and now that relief has been granted, one may doubt if the farmers have really been purged by suffering. But two facts are undeniable, first that there were some years during which the intelligent farmers could make profits only by hard thinking while the majority lost because tradition for them had taken the place of thought : and second, necessity having been the midwife to new methods, agriculture has become more enterprising and more efficient as a result of its troubles.

It would be tedious to examine again the reasons why British agriculture found itself in a mess during the later 'twenties and the earlier 'thirties. Some were forces that the farmers could not control and others were facts that they did not want to understand. In general it may be said that they were facing the problems of 1926 with the mentality of 1900. The result was unpleasant for all who depended on agri-culture. Men were paid off. Arable land was put down to grass. There seemed to be no hope except in generous subsidies from the State. For the next few years the farmers survived in an alternation of hope and despair, each in the middle of his little desert that one day might blossom again under a shower of subsidies and gentle tariff dews.

Scottish farmers deserve great praise for the way they maintained their farms during those bad years—especially in the light of what happened to England. The English farmer has always been more of a gent. than the Scotsman. He enjoyed the increase of a richer soil : his fathers had enjoyed it for generations before him : and he had a tradition of greater ease than we have known, except perhaps in the Lothians. When prices finally collapsed after the War, many of those proud yeomen were so completely surprised that they could not understand what had happened : and even when they did get some idea of their real condition, they were so accustomed to an easy life that they could not adapt themselves to hard work and bare living.

The landlords could not help them either. In England, as in Scotland, many landlords took advantage of boom conditions to sell out their farms, and the tenants had either to buy, or leave a place where their family had lived for generations. Mortgages, lightly undertaken in 1920, were a dreadful burden by 1926, when the value of land and stock had fallen. Landlords who had already sold could not be expected to help the buyers : and the landlords who retained their estates had neither the money nor the knowledge (nor, in some cases, the inclination) to help their tenants in difficulties. Thus, hundreds of square miles of good farming land gradually deteriorated, all over England. Farms in Dorset that used to grow wheat and mutton have gone down to foul grass, on which a few dairy cows exist half by the mercy of heaven and half by the grace of the Milk Marketing Board. So in other counties. It will take years to repair that loss.

That did not happen in Scotland. The Scottish farmer had no long tradition of easy living, and when the bad times came, it was easier for him to adapt himself. He had the same handicaps as the Englishman —farms bought too dear ; impoverished, inefficient or indifferent landlords ; uneconomic methods and foreign competition. Feeling the draught, he cried as loudly for the Government blanket. But he did also try to save himself.

The Scottish farmers at their best were not more intelligent than the best of Englishmen. It would be a very wrong thing to give the impression that English agriculture went into total eclipse in the late 'twenties. On the contrary, the best English farmers developed new methods that the times demanded and Scottish farmers are in debt to them for ideas and examples. The difference between the two countries was this— while English farming at its best may have been even more advanced than the best in Scotland, the general average in Scotland may have been slightly higher.

Bad times made the Scottish farmers work hard to get the most out of their land by the old methods and forced them to consider anything new that might help them. Thus, while England came through the troubles with a big loss, Scotland in 1935 was probably better farmed than ever before. It was a triumph of training and temperament, and it may be seen best of all in the numbers of young Scotsmen who have gone to East Anglia and Essex and prospered there by hard work, in holdings abandoned by their English tenants, in despair.

It is nothing to be particularly proud of that we know how to work hard, because we are poor. But it is a fact that has had some importance for Scottish farming.

A few figures will show the increasing efficiency of Scottish agriculture. Though the extent of arable land has decreased by 15 per cent. since the end of the War, we have 13 per cent. more milk cows, 15 per cent. more beef cattle, 20 per cent. more sheep and 70 per cent. more poultry. Pigs have also increased, but the trade is liable to violent fluctuations. It is also important to notice that since farmers are selling fat cattle at a much earlier age than they used to, the overturn is now much quicker. Barley shows an increase of a quarter to the acre and oats an increase of slightly more. Potato crops also have improved, by about a ton an acre. Thus the ing produce true of the d more re- re has been porary legs. plough need d could not give a reasonable return in arable cultivation. It is better to fully exploit the good than to break our hearts upon the stony limits.

The immediate history of agriculture falls into two parts—the development in technique made by the individual farmers to retain their place in the market and the legislative measures designed to control the intense individualism among the members of the industry.

It would be too much to say that the tractor was a result of the depression, for the tractor was only another stage in something that has been going on for 150 years.

ERRATUM

Page 101, line 20
For "legs" read "leys"

Nor, I think, was it the most remarkable application of machines to agriculture. The invention of the reaper, the self-binder, and the threshing mill that did away with so much casual labour would have had far more effect on rural economy. The tractor was being adopted slowly in Scotland and that process would have gone on but it was greatly accelerated by the depression : until horses are now fewer by a third. On a farm of three pairs of horses and upwards, the tractor could take the place of two pairs of work horses, and perhaps make possible the cultivation of more land. Therefore many farmers that had enterprise and some capital (or credit) bought tractors and accelerated the still further mechanisation of their industry.

Not all of them found the tractors a complete success. Ploughmen who understood the curious nature of a horse had less sympathy with a beast of steel that fed on paraffin. Though they could spend hours grooming their pair, they had no taste for cleaning the innards of a motor. Thus the machines were not kept in the best running order ; they often broke down, and their owners condemned them as uneconomic.

Implements were also a problem. A farmer who had excellent equipment for horses found it was not suitable for the tractor. When he bought tractor implements, he might find them unsuitable for his type of land. Then again, there was an idea that tractors could be used only in big fields of flat land free from stones. So mechanisation was suspect by the more conservative and taken up and then dropped by the others who had not the right kind of temperament.

But farmers with a mechanical mind set out to learn the new technique and very soon enlarged our ideas of what tractors could do. These mechanics proved that the agricultural mind can adapt itself when it likes. First of all they learned how to use and care for the machines, and which machines were more suitable for their type of land. Then they began to experiment with implements, adapting them also to their own particular needs. Some of the most advanced (" naething but damned engineers ") very soon proved, to their own satisfaction, that the tractor could do any job and could be adapted for any ground worth cultivation. There were others who would not believe that : not even when they saw it proved before their own eyes.

Two other arguments used against the tractors were disproved.

It was said they would mean a great decrease in the number of ploughmen. That seems to depend on the circumstances of the farm. In one case, a rich farm on the remains of the old red sandstone, where all the horses had been sold and only tractors used, production has been very greatly increased and the number of men employed has been doubled. That could not have been done by the use of horses : or, if it could, the risks would have been appalling in a wet fall. There is no doubt that, given a sane economic order, tractors would increase production enormously without driving a single man off the land.

The second argument was that the ploughmen would not learn to use the tractors. That was quite wrong. Some men were so fond of their old ways that they could not abide the machines and would take lower wages so that they could go on ploughing with the horses. But farmers that were enthusiastic about tractors and understood them have had no difficulty in training their men. Now there are thousands of men that have become so keen on tractors that they would rather leave the land than return to horses. They are experts in handling their machines, use up a lot of their spare time cleaning their motors, and have all the pride that the old ploughman was supposed to have in his pair. They even take the tractors to ploughing matches, thus spoiling the day for the sound traditionalists ; and fifty machines competed in a power ploughing match near Laurencekirk in the Mearns in January of this year. Thus the countryside changes : till the oil salesman is almost as notable a figure in some districts as the horse-dealer was when I was a child.

The opponents of the tractor said it was making the farm into a factory. That phrase might be used for other tendencies in agriculture during and since the depression. The ideal in all industries has been to get the largest production in the smallest possible time, and to hell with quality. Agriculture has had to follow that ideal. Fortunately those methods do not apply very well when used on growing things, and the factory style of production that some thought the way to fortune has brought several disasters and leaves some hard problems to be solved.

All other production being speeded up, farmers tried to speed up the cow and the hen. The cow, that used to be a friend of the family and lived in a back room off the kitchen, was turned into a machine for the producing of milk. So much food and water was fed into her, and so much milk was drawn off three times a day. Everything possible was done by scientific breeding and feeding to increase that yield of milk. Provided the milk showed the standard amount of butter-fat no one worried about the quality of the increased yield : indeed it was hardly desirable, in this mad world, to keep a cow that gave a small yield of rich milk, unless hers could be used to standardise the vast quantities of watery liquid produced by her copious sisters. But even machines, if driven too hard, give out. The over-exploited cows became more and more susceptible to disease. Contagious abortion reduced the farmer's profits, and now mastitis, an infection of the mammary system, is reducing them further. Only scientists can say why these troubles should increase, and the scientists, having been wrong so often, are unwilling to guess. But it is reasonable inference that a beast weakened by over-production has not the strength to resist disease. The factory method has its dangers.

The hen, that has suffered even more than the cow, is an even better example. The improvers were not content with breeding hens to give 200 eggs in a laying period. They divorced the birds entirely from their traditional way of living. Hatched in incubators they were brought up in foster-mothers and then transferred to battery layers. There, in a wire cage in an air-conditioned shed, they had nothing to do but eat their ration and lay their daily egg, or be fattened for the market. In order to compensate for lack of sunshine they were given a weekly dose of oil. It was a fearful violence to condemn the hen, a creature of infinite activity, to such a life of dullness. But nature, distorted, had its revenge. Either the artificial conditions, or the over-production of eggs, or both together, weakened the stock. Bacillary white diarrhœa and then fowl paralysis meant the loss of millions of birds and thousands of pounds in a few years. Breeders are now being forced to allow their chickens the liberty of the fields, in the hope of strengthening their stock. They are also beginning to think that the hen who conserves her strength and lays a modest total pays better than the zealous bird that dies of over-production. There is, it seems, a danger of improving in too great a hurry.

These, then, were the methods employed by farmers to make up for the fall in prices—mechanisation and increased production. They had their successes and they brought their problems. In so far as they were used with intelligence and moderation they were good things. But they were not enough to bring back prosperity. Something had to be done on the marketing side.

The farmers thought the marketing problem had an easy and obvious solution—that miraculous cure for all industrial ills, a straight tariff. Let the Government impose such duties as would raise the price of home-grown food to a level that would give a sure and substantial profit, and Scotland would be full of milk and honey again. That solution, however desirable, was not as easy as it looked : for, if the price of food were raised, consumers might not be able to buy the milk and honey, unless their wages were raised in proportion. So, while waiting, and agitating, for tariffs, the leaders of the industry, who have much more intelligence than their followers, tried some reorganisation, based on an appeal to reason.

It was obvious that agriculture suffered through the individualism of its units and that thousands of small producers, each acting on his own, were easy game for the dealers. If these would stand by collective agreements, much better terms could be got from the distributors. The milk farmers in the West of Scotland made various experiments with co-operative creameries and collective bargaining with the milk distributors and finally set up the Scottish Milk Marketing agency, a voluntary association which tried to regulate the marketing of milk for the whole of the west. This was successful enough to show that statutory powers would be needed for compelling the eternal minority into the scheme. The ground was thus prepared for the Marketing Boards, which, planned by a Labour Government, were set up by a National one and have imposed a certain order upon industry by limiting the farmer's power to bargain as he pleases.

What has been the effect of the Marketing Boards ? They have raised and stabilised the prices that the farmer gets for milk and potatoes and thus far they are a good thing. But they are perhaps not so good from the consumer's point of view, for they have not touched the distributive agencies with their excessive costs : and until they do there will always be a chance for critics to say that they are only price-raising schemes. They should not be dismissed so lightly : they have helped the producers, and they are an admission that order is necessary. It only remains to extend that order.

A great deal has been done for agriculture since the Labour Government drew up the first Marketing Bills. The Sugar Beet subsidy (a previous measure) has been a perpetual sweetmeat. The Wheat Quota has been of great assistance in England. A subsidy has been given for meat. And now the Government are giving grants for the liming and manuring of the land. Add to these the fact that farmers have been relieved of seven-eighths of their local rates, and if the total does not come very near prosperity then agriculture must be in a very deplorable state. Fortunately it isn't. One hears of farmers who made a profit of 30, 40 and 50 per cent. on their capital last year, and while these are exceptionally good returns they are an indication that circumstances have improved tremendously. There has been a price for that change. Marketing Boards, restrictions, rules, questionnaires, acres of buff, pink, blue, green and white forms, official curiosity—the farmers have had to submit to them all ; and you can realise that the men who ordinarily would not have told even their wives (let alone the Inland Revenue) how much they were making, resent that interference with their own business. Some of them still regard all that has been done for them as the devil's tricks and sigh for that fine straight tariff. But others are well enough content. They should be.

There is another way in which the farmers are being asked to give a *quid pro quo* : in this case a rather small *quid* for a very substantial *quo*. It was understood that help received from the State should be passed on in some small measure to the workers. Since emigration stopped ten years ago and unemployment increased in the towns, young men could not escape from the countryside. That gave the farmers an advantage in the labour market. Wages, always low, grew smaller. Therefore, when the farmer's living had been assured, the Agricultural Wages (Regulation) Scotland Act was passed last year and eleven committees have been set up to fix minimum wages for the labourers. It is too soon to say anything more about these. Meantime, however, the boom in urban trades has given the farm-worker his traditional escape from the land. Ploughmen and labourers are so scarce that farmers have had to pay higher wages and so the farmers are having to give the *quid pro quo* without action by the Boards. The Boards will likely be most useful in a time of declining prosperity.

Agriculture is prosperous, but one may doubt if it has really solved its problems yet. There is the question of labour. Rural conditions are not good enough to keep the best men on the land. The wages are on the small side : and the houses are too often unattractive. The tied-cottar house (the house that goes with the job, and must be vacated at the end of the agreement) is a bad thing : even the Government is against it. Too many of these houses are in a disgraceful condition : and even when they are reconstructed, many are undesirable because of their awkward or lonely positions at the back of turnip fields or near the sides of middens. Baths are not thought necessary, because of course the men work so much in the rain.

The reconstructed houses are an immense improvement on the old ones but they have two disadvantages— they give no security of tenure and they are not as modern as council houses in the town. These two facts decrease their usefulness by half because the best men (influenced by their wives) will not stay on the land when they can get better houses with security of tenure elsewhere. Therefore it is to be hoped that the County Councils will support the Government's official policy and build many thousands of good modern houses in small communities on convenient sites, and will, as far as possible, discourage the tied-house system. For only urban standards of living will keep the best men on the land. That may be deplorable : in an ideal world, the labourer would put public duty before self-interest : but as long as the farmers demand even a decreasing self-determination and free choice, the labourers will need to get the same.

The problem of prosperity still remains. Can the Marketing Boards, the quotas, subsidies and tariffs ensure permanent prosperity ? That has to be decided. They will do well enough as long as urban industries are busy. But what will happen if the consumers' money contracts instead of expanding ? There is a reason for thinking we are not at the end of the changes. When a Conservative ex-Minister of Agriculture like the late Lord Ernle and an expert like Mr C. S. Orwin think nationalisation of the land is highly desirable, or even inevitable, we may anticipate something of the sort in the next hundred years. And if nationalisation of the land—what else ? Perhaps those are right who see the farmer as a tortured saint sitting on the thin ends of a hundred wedges. Agriculture has had to change its way to save itself : likely it will have to go on changing if it is to survive in a prosperous way. Individualism may have to accept much more drastic limitations if a highly organised community is going to develop. And it is no argument that you can't change human nature. The change is not necessary. Human nature need only be modified, a little at a time ; and that can be done, else the Shorthorn breeders of Aberdeenshire would still be chasing the wild rams on Bennachie, painted with woad and clad in lousy sheepskins.

HOUSES OF THE PEOPLE

by
GEORGE SCOTT-MONCRIEFF

Do you like old houses built in the traditional style of a country? There are still many such in Scotland: and Mr Scott-Moncrieff tells you where some of the best can be found

THE OLD HOUSES

NOWADAYS it is difficult to believe that in the eighteenth century Glasgow was the most beautiful city in Scotland. Many travellers sang the praises of her towers and steeples rising above the gently flowing Clyde. Almost everything has been obliterated ; the new Glasgow was a mushroom city that rose at an unfortunate time. The Cathedral huddles in the shadow of barracks of masonry, for it was not considered worthy of any considerable open space. The splendid seventeenth century University was pulled down some years ago, it is said because the wives of the professors objected to living near the adjacent slums. "Any other city," a present-day professor has remarked, "would have pulled down the slums. Glasgow . . . ! "

Edinburgh was more fortunate, for her expansion was carried out, not on a wave of big-business but while eighteenth century ideas of quality, spaciousness, and taste still held. So, a windowed Colosseum, Moray Place rings round its trees and grass circle while the sun passes from pillar to pillar. Charlotte Square, despite some nasty swellings in part of its roof-line, remains to delight. George Street, for a few more years at least until the ostentation of bank and insurance company takes full effect, is a constant pleasure. The romantic panorama south of Princes Street blinds us to the gimcrack jumble of its horrid shops. Despite the efforts of successive Town Councils the Old Town has still some really fine buildings, admirably suited to the quick descent of the High Street and the Canongate. Not that Edinburgh has cause for pride of late, she has exuded foul suburbs. Nor can bloating Glasgow be said to have made any serious effort at redeeming herself from the charge of little relieved ugliness.

But it is not with the present but with the past that we are momentarily concerned. A culture emerges from geographical and racial peculiarities. In prehistoric times the elusive Pict built himself his dun, or broch. These brochs may be seen from Shetland to Berwickshire and nowhere else in the world. Only that at Mousa is substantially complete, a great hollow tower built to some fifty feet, slightly tapering, the wall itself hollow with a low-stepped stair winding to the summit. Many of the brochs are built of enormous shaped stones, which proved their ruin as subsequent generations made quarries of them. They were strongholds, the tribes could shelter in them with their beasts and they could from the top see the approach of enemies at a great distance. To-day their tumbled stones have a relevance to rough countryside.

Perhaps the brochs were still in use when, in 397, St Ninian built his church on the Isle of Whithorn. Nothing remains of his *Candida Casa*, although the shell of a later chapel is there, and nearby the ruins of the Priory Church that was built seven hundred years later and to which the Scottish kings made regular pilgrimage. In his native Ireland the building of churches flourished, but in Scotland St Ninian's mission was not of itself to bring widespread conversion ; although there was a slow

infiltration of missionaries it was not until St Columba
came to Iona that even the most primitive of chapels
and cells were built in any number. Their larochs
stand in the Isles and on the west coast. That of
St Maelrubha, the red-tonsured, in Applecross looks out
over the red bay and the blue outline of Skye, although
almost all the carved stones were smashed by priest-
ridden crofters of the nineteenth century Presbyterian
revival. There are at Brechin and Abernethy round
towers of the Irish type ; graceful stacks, built separate
from the church and used by the clergy as the Picts
had used their brochs, as strongholds and outlook towers.
But the Scottish towers do not date from before 1000,
the end of which century saw the building of the first
Abbey in Scotland, Dunfermline, founded by Queen
Margaret, although the lovely nave, the oldest remaining
portion, is not actually of the original fabric but dates
from about 1130, about the same time as the first of
the Border Abbeys were being built at Kelso and
Jedburgh. More fortunate than any of these churches,
the Cathedral of St Magnus, in the Orkneys, is to-day
intact. Its great red romanesque arches tower through
the narrow nave, their red shadows give vastness to
what is in fact small and slender. In Glasgow, the only
other of the early Cathedrals remaining (Iona was not
made a Cathedral until 1507, and St Giles only after
the Reformation), Gothic in Scotland may be seen at
its finest.

The earliest of our castles were Norman, built
chiefly of wood on mounds specified as " motes,"
protected by earthworks more or less regular in type.
Naturally, the actual woodwork has not withstood man
and time, but foundations may be traced and there are
early pictures that show the elevations. As offensive

weapons and methods were developed, and fire was used to shorten sieges, woodwork, even when daubed deep in clay, became no longer an adequate protection. By the thirteenth century castles of stone were going up, very often on the motes themselves. Some of these earlier castles retain the primitive form of their wooden precursors although most have undergone so many subsequent alterations as to obliterate their origins from all but expert eyes. The older castles include Castle Duffus, Castle Campbell, Dirleton, Dunstaffnage, Tantallon, Caerlaverock, Kildrummy, and Bothwell on the Clyde.

If the older fabrics are in varying stages of ruin, there are still in Scotland a number of later castles and towers in the full beauty of their original form. In Aberdeenshire they are to be seen at their boldest and most elaborate, the original functions of fortifications half-developed into decoration, not, as in the baronial revival, applied and ridiculous ornament, but intrinsic, only treated with the abandon permissible to a more peaceful age : Midmar the magnificent with all its turrets tumbled into an unexpected conformity ; Castle Fraser, not quite so successful as a whole but rich in the detail of its delicately projected turrets ; Allardyce with its deep diced corbelling ; Crathes, Craigievar, and Castle Barra. Slighter but comparable is Rowallan in Ayrshire, intact but now empty and neglected.

Very different is Borthwick in the Lothians, vast twin pillars of pale stone split by a shaft of shadow, ornamented only by heavy machicolations beneath the parapet. Borthwick is of ashlar, but those Scottish buildings which are of rubble were usually intended to be harled and whitewashed, sometimes with ashlar turrets projecting and contrasting : the present fetish for picking out the harling and treating the rubble like crazy paving is to be regretted.

Castle Stewart, Dundarave, well restored by Lorimer, Kilcoy in the Black Isle, also well restored, and Barcaldine, are fine structures that represent a less ornate transition from castle to mansion. Many of such buildings have been developed around original towers, but there are a number of towers, some dating from as late as the seventeenth century, which have never been expanded. Coxton in Moray shows to a nicety the merit of whitewashed harling. Craigcaffie in Galloway, a short tower with parapets only on two sides, a steep roof pitch and crow-stepped gables, is a late building, the last stage of fortification merging into the first of the small Scottish house, a most pleasing whole. Neglected Midhope on the Forth has a fine arched gateway. On the Border there is Smailholm, and Kirkhope, poor Kirkhope amongst the heather; you will stand in it deep amongst the doos' droppings and look up through the floorless walls to where eighteenth century fireplaces hang and the sky shows through the hollow windows. Soon the roof will go and the walls moither away; Kirkhope will join our heritage of ruin.

It is time for a diatribe against ruins. Scotland is full of them, and seems fuller than she actually is. All summer long the people walk wondering behind uniformed guides through the stark ribs of Dryburgh and Melrose, and around them the guide endeavours to reconstruct a great church for the piety of the tourist. We are proud of our ruins where we ought to be ashamed of them. Sure, ruins have their place; they are well adapted for meditation upon the transience of things; for the archæologist they present delightful clues for detection. They often give charm, if of a sentimental character, depending rather upon association than upon form, to the landskip. But they are not as their builders conceived them, the vandals have shared in their creation and they retain the ethos of the breaker as well as of the maker.

St Andrews capitalises her Cathedral, which is merely a serration of stone tusks before which the aching imagination sinks, incapable of visualising a great church, overwhelmed with thought of the state of a land that brought so much to nothing. Yet for years St Andrews has been pulling down buildings that, if without the erstwhile magnificence of the Cathedral, are beautiful, do maintain a rich native tradition, and are far more serviceable than their wretched successors. These houses, forming the wide pleasant streets that constitute the real charm of the town, date from the sixteenth, seventeenth, and eighteenth centuries. They are the heritors of that tradition of Scottish architecture which, in the case of the mansion, was untimely interrupted by the incoming of the classical. Queen Mary's House is the most elaborate; it has a tower wing at the back, vaulted ground floor and panelled rooms. In South Street there are several groups of grand four-storeyed houses, in at least one of which an enterprising householder has recently discovered painted ceilings of the old Scottish type beneath later plaster. Then there are a number of little two-flatted houses with outside stairs, typical of much of that fast-disappearing cottage tradition of the south-east. However, there is some hope for St Andrews, for her citizens have recently formed a Preservation Trust.

The architecture of the old Scottish burgh may be seen at its best in the Fife coast towns : crow-stepped gables on well-proportioned, solid houses, roofed with pantiles, their lintels carved with initials, date, and emblem, forming curving streets that slope to the harbour and the sea-front. These houses, the tolbooths, the mercat crosses and the doocots, would, if they had the significance they should have for Scots, surely influence us to better things in these days of rebuilding. Big shops are erected in the flashy, cardboard tradition that is in the worst sense international : inns and teashops bedizen themselves with imitation half-timbering : council houses are grim boxes daubed with dirt-coloured cement-harling. We do not wish to return to the baronial revival, when it was considered that a corbelled turret made a house traditional and such turrets were stuck on at the most laughable projections. No one regrets the classical era that gave us the fine buildings of Bruce, the Adams, Playfair, but it should not act as an insuperable barrier to our taking up again the unexhausted tradition of earlier times, the essential simplicity of which lends itself admirably to the needs of the day.

Likewise, the Scottish village has been unjustly neglected, and is in consequence now being rebuilt with no discrimination. Our villages are varied and suited to their landskips : along Tayside there are reed-thatched houses, in Galloway they are commonly whitewashed, with small thick slates. In the Lothians there are some lovely villages built of soft-coloured stone, slated and pantiled, often embracing fine old churches.

Architecture is the most immediate evidence of a national culture. When we pay due respect to what we have, both as regards its care and its emulation, there will be more hope for us.

by
ROBERT HURD

In the following piece a practising architect, whose broad but unashamed nationalism distresses the elderly members of his profession, discusses the tendencies of our modern Scottish architecture

DESIGN FOR TO-DAY

CASTING a superficial eye over Scotland, even an observant visitor might be forgiven for concluding that modern architecture had not yet reached this country. There is indeed no dearth of post-War building, but in design much of it is too timid or commonplace to have recognisable character.

Not that Scotland is constitutionally incapable of producing pioneer architecture. By no means ! That herald of modernism, Charles Rennie Mackintosh, not only came out of Scotland, but throve on her best native traditions and did most of his few works in his own country. He is unique in that he alone seemed to appreciate (without actually saying so) that the traditional spirit of Scottish architecture had a message for to-day ; and by his work and the contribution he thereby made to European architecture of the twentieth century he might be said to have repaid partly the debt owed by Scotland to the Continent for all she received from France and the Low Countries in the sixteenth and seventeenth centuries.

Of what does this essential traditional spirit consist ? I would say bold simplicity threaded by an odd streak of vanity. Take any Scottish domestic building of the most national period round about 1600. The simple structure in stone rubble is made exciting by the daring

Design for To-day : Westquarter—A Re-Housing Scheme near Falkirk

DESIGN FOR TO-DAY : The Glasgow College of Art

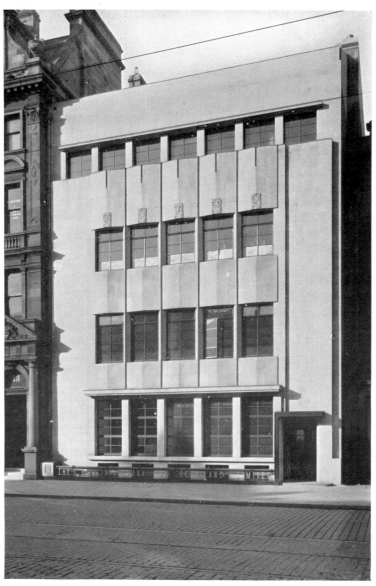

DESIGN FOR TO-DAY: A Bank in George Street, Edinburgh

Design for To-day : A Block of Flats in Edinburgh

projection of turrets and corbels which occur, not for the external display of some conceit, but to satisfy an internal need, maybe a dressing-closet or stair, so placed as not to interrupt the square shape of the main rooms. There were inevitably certain details of period significance, such as crow-steps, ornamental dormer windows displaying family heraldry and monograms, national emblems and dates, elaborate doorways and wrought-iron balustrades ; but these do not concern us here. The main point is that external symmetry and balanced façade were of quite secondary importance to internal convenience.

The relation between this Scots tradition and modernism is now clear. During the nineteenth century and even later this was, however, by no means so. The paraphernalia of " period " obscured appreciation of essentials, and many Victorian buildings such as Balmoral, Kinnettles, or large tenement developments in the Warrender district of Edinburgh, display an almost comic loyalty to this fustian. I have often felt that the climax must surely have been reached in a certain old lowland house to which, in Victorian times, the owner had added a "bachelors' " wing. Inevitably it had a turret, and this turret had large windows all round and in the centre a bath in which the bachelors were expected to wash *coram populo*. This baronial style became a hall-mark of county status : the "odd streak of vanity " indeed dominated architecture in Victorian Scotland !

Genuine research into the craftsmanship of the Scots tradition was begun by Sir Rowand Anderson and continued by others, principally Sir Robert Lorimer. The latter achieved a real revival of Scottish feeling in building, but he did not carry on from that to develop a native modern idiom, and his work, though abundant, various and often pleasing, cannot therefore be said to be of European importance. But his name is enshrined as architect of the National War Memorial at Edinburgh Castle, a building which (perhaps significantly) has been a genuine popular success though it is by no means his best work.

Meanwhile, what of Charles Rennie Mackintosh— what had he done ? Between 1894 and 1904 he built the Glasgow School of Art, a building which aroused enthusiasm in Europe, but not apparently, in Scotland. The Glasgow School of Art is by no means perfect, but it dares greatly (consider for one moment the period in which it was built) and in a way which one frankly admits defies definition, is clearly Scottish. Perhaps it is the height of the building on a steeply sloping site, perhaps it is the relation of wall spaces to window spaces, or perhaps it is the silhouette seen from the corner of Scott Street and Sauchiehall Street—I do not know ; but others outside Scotland share this opinion. It certainly embodies our tradition of bold simplicity. And how dully pompous beside it appears the Edinburgh College of Art with its classical impedimenta and arid expanses of roof! This comparison perhaps reveals more fully than anything else the free yet basically Scottish character of Mackintosh's work.

Mackintosh's frankly functional attitude to design was fully appreciated abroad, particularly in Austria ; but apart from a fleeting influence on office façades in Glasgow he had hardly any influence in Scotland at all. I am told by Mackintosh's contemporaries in Glasgow that his work was the occasion of much hilarity there at the time (about 1900), and it is significant that the only publication about his work is No. 2 of *Meister*

Der Innen Kunst, published over thirty years ago by Koch of Darmstadt and now practically unobtainable ; also that apart from the Mitchell Library in Glasgow no Public Library in Scotland had this book until in 1936 the National Library was persuaded to buy it !

There are at present two major influences affecting our architecture, the use of building materials (mainly bricks) and methods of construction new to Scotland, and the tendency of builders and architects to ignore Scottish traditions. The first effects of these influences are not encouraging ; but there are signs that design is beginning to resolve itself into something vaguely recognisable as a native idiom. This development is not caused by a harking back to old forms but by the influence primarily of climate and secondly of scenic background. Put baldly this means that boisterous weather places distinct limits on the adoption of southern types of building and that Nature's quiet tones in Scotland do not receive harsh southern colours happily. Technically, of course, there are further tendencies in the same direction—the unsuitability of English cavity walls and so on, but these need not concern us here.

While we may be beginning to find our feet, the enormous crop of bungalows that has sprung up around many Scottish towns has struck an alien note that will continue to displease until these flimsy structures go the way of all cheap building in a rigorous climate. The ideal form of dwelling for Scottish towns is the flat : our ancestors discovered that in the sixteenth century. It beats the weather, allows for our gregarious habits and tramples on social distinctions. Proper planning of a residential district on these lines gives in addition more open space for recreation and clothes-drying than a whole suburb of bungalows (*vide* Stockholm). The basic wisdom of this Scottish tradition has been forcibly brought home in late years by the acute shortage of good houses in the centre of cities near places of work. Scottish workers do not like being satellited to the outskirts ; and if for a time they dallied with the idea after the War, they seem to be discovering its disadvantages now.

Post-War architecture in Scotland will be mainly notable for the enormous bulk of new State-assisted housing. Much of it is mediocre, some of it bad, and a little very good indeed. The new housing in Dunbartonshire, for instance, is first-class : the plans are good, the general layout is spacious and the external appearance in sympathy with its background. Another good scheme, in this case to rehouse miners, is at Westquarter in Stirlingshire ; and a third, more urban in character, is now being built at Peterhead. Judging from the drawings this last will demonstrate effectively just how good a properly designed tenement of flats can be.

Why is it that more good examples do not exist ? The reasons are not far to seek. Firstly, the members of local housing authorities do not as a rule know much about design (good or bad) and it follows that, secondly, they are not really capable of choosing the right man as housing architect or criticising his work afterwards. The lack of good town-planning in modern Scotland— Aberdeen is an exception—is due to the same causes ; why else, for instance, should Edinburgh have a good town - planning school in its midst while the city authorities muddle on complacently with no proper development plan for the city—for Edinburgh, of all places ?

The churches have been more progressive than the

local authorities, and the Church of Scotland has at last been making some attempt to face up to the type of church required for Presbyterian worship. Lately the needs of new housing areas have caused the building of several good churches and church halls, which are mostly faced outside with stone. The new Roman Catholic churches in Highland districts are a welcome change from the pseudo-Gothic buildings associated with post-emancipation Catholicism in Scotland, for they are simple stone — sometimes even granite — structures with white interiors and a minimum of ornament. One of the best small ones is at Roy Bridge in Inverness-shire, but curiously enough their most striking granite church is designed by a London architect ; at Oban he has really achieved a modern development of the Scots tradition in the new Catholic Cathedral for Argyll and Isles.

Up to post-War years Scottish roads were not suited to modern traffic demands, and since then therefore there has been a big programme of road construction, accompanied inevitably by the making of many new bridges. By way of contrast with the general run of architecture, modern bridges in Scotland are nearly all interesting. The tradition of good bridge building established two hundred years ago by Wade has not been disgraced ; nor has the love of experiment displayed in Telford's work or in the Forth Bridge been forsaken — witness the interesting series of concrete bridges sponsored by the Inverness County Council and the Ministry of Transport on the Great North Road and in the Great Glen. The bridges between Fort William and Inverness are particularly good as modern developments of the simple Wade tradition.

Students of modern industrial and commercial architecture cannot learn much from Scotland. A country does not experience prolonged depression and at the same time see the erection of many new factories and business premises. Possibly the new industrial estate at Hillington may see some interesting experiments in factory design, but it is too early yet to pass judgment. There have, however, been several good pit-head baths of simple functional design in the mining areas, and the Scottish banks have lately built several massive offices in Glasgow and one of them has recently started a new head office in Edinburgh. Banks, however, are rarely adventurous, and these pseudo-classical offices are obviously influenced by the American conception of the bank as a Temple of Finance. But to this generalisation Edinburgh provides one exception which, though not perfect, is nevertheless too remarkable to be ignored. The temporary headquarters of the National Bank of Scotland in George Street is a frankly modern office building of modest proportions and refinement : that in itself is rare enough in business circles to be notable : but, *mirabile dictu*, we actually see here a belated development of C. R. Mackintosh's work. And the same firm has more recently produced an equally modest but more severe shop-building in between two rather flowery essays in Renascence architecture at the east end of Princes Street. One can only hope that both these buildings are signs of the times.

It has been suggested that the modernist design of the Empire Exhibition at Bellahouston should stimulate a wider appreciation of modern architecture in Scotland. The general impression conveyed by the Exhibition buildings is one of modern Dutch efficiency. (I would except from this the Imperial Chemicals Pavilion—

a vigorously exotic building that looks like being the best in the Exhibition.) Modern Dutch architecture is good, and it is possible that once again Scotland is to receive influences from the Low Countries. Exhibition buildings, however, can hardly have much effect on our domestic architecture, the sphere in which most development is likely to take place during the next ten years owing to the housing shortage. But perhaps the shock effect of the Exhibition will help us to have a proper appreciation of Mackintosh, our own pioneer.

In closing, one may properly urge that the basic need to-day is to rescue Scotland from the imminent threat of provincialism, an evil that stifles all healthy indigenous growth. Only by encouraging new architecture native to Scotland, while at the same time developing direct cultural contacts between Scotland and the Continent, can we hope to raise the standard of taste and appreciation from its present low level. Timidity, plausibly disguised as caution, is significantly prevalent in modern Scottish architecture ; significantly because architecture is a reliable mirror of a country's condition—and above all is it essential that we should throw off our fear of experiment and independence.

EDUCATION

A SYSTEM AND ITS FRUITS

by
J. R. PEDDIE, C.B.E., D.Litt.

The Scottish educational system has long been admired as one of the finest in the world. Here an expert describes the beauty of its parts and the way they fit together

THE SYSTEM

THE publications of His Majesty's Government, known familiarly as " Blue Books," are not uncommonly treated as matters for jest : the popular belief is that they are the supreme harbourers of dust since, once they are placed on the shelf, none ever wants to move them again. Whatever be the truth of the matter in regard to these bulky volumes in general, it is, in the case of school education in Scotland, essential, indeed praiseworthy, to blow the dust from the records of the Scottish Education Department, embodied in the annual reports, for only by a survey of them can one hope to maintain one's perspective, to gauge the measure of achievement and to appreciate the rise and development of new ideals.

There is in Scotland a peculiarly depressing kind of individual who tells you that " things are not what they were." Through the mists of the mind of such an one the " old days " appear tinged with the golden light of sheer intellectualism. Teachers were great and formidable figures, remarkable for their eccentricities, fit material for story and reminiscence : the " lads o' pairts " swarmed to the universities and, in the teeth of the severest odds, won through to brilliant success in life : even the school-room, the desk, deeply and impressively incised by the initials of the afterwards

famous, became subjects for romance. We can all
fill in fuller details of this picture.

Now it is no wish of mine to pour scorn on the sentimentality that encompasses the mental make-up of the
pessimist of whom I have written above. But if one
wishes to present a true picture of Scottish education
to-day it is only by looking at past records with some
care that one can separate fact from fiction, and, in a
mood of realism, endeavour to show how great the
advance has been. There is no person engaged on the
actual administration of Scottish education to-day who
would wish to detract in the slightest degree from the
great fundamental features of the system so nobly
enshrined in John Knox's *Book of Discipline*. Tribute
must be paid to the magnificent work done obscurely
in parish schools, to the fierce joy which selected scholars
took in the acquisition of knowledge, partly for its own
sake and partly for the position it would enable them to
take in the pulpit, the school-room, the court of law, or
by the bedside of the sick. Emphasis, too, must be laid
on the fact that poverty has never, in Scotland, been
regarded as a barrier to the highest forms of education
which the country could offer. These things we can
hold in reverence. But if, because of them, we persist
in the belief that the simplicity and narrowness of
Scottish education in the past yielded results incompar-
ably better than those nowadays achieved, we shall
stand convicted of an obscurantism which, when faced
with the tremendous educational activity of the present
time, will become merely ludicrous.

Perhaps the most striking way in which to mark
the advance of recent years is to consider the child in
the school environment. I write, not of private or
fee-paying schools, but of the ordinary school adminis-

tered by the statutory authority, the Education Committee of the Town or County Council.

The school of even sixty years ago was not, prevailingly, a pretty place. Frequently the children were seated at long desks in badly-lit and dingily painted rooms. On the walls were maps, many of them depressing in the extreme. The playground received scant attention. Anything would do. The sanitary arrangements were unpleasant and often primitive. The children, if it was a school in a poor quarter, were less well clad than they now are. No provision was made for feeding them or clothing them. None bothered to look at their teeth. Their general dietary was in the lap of the gods, their physical health haphazardly tended. Truancy was not uncommon, being the direct result of the general attitude towards the school as a whole on the part of those sturdy rebels who could never be got to believe that the school was going to do them any good.

It would be absurd to say that all this is swept away. But the effort completely to remove the bad school never ceases. Since the War every Scottish Education Authority, in greater or less degree, has striven to house its school children in buildings that are calculated to bring health and happiness. I wonder how many parents of an older generation have any conception of the immense change that has come upon the school scene. In the modern schools now springing up in every locality the building is so adjusted as to get the maximum of sunlight. Warmth and ventilation are matters to which the utmost technical skill is devoted. Class-rooms and corridors are brightly painted, pictures of interest, vivid and arresting, hang on the walls, while every effort is made to ensure ease of working on the part of the teacher by the provision of blackboards and other necessities of school life which are at once efficient and unobtrusive.

To go fully into all the modern requirements for the medical and dental inspection of children, the feeding and clothing of those poorly circumstanced, the milk-supply given daily at fractional cost or at no cost at all, the attention given to physical exercises and to games would require more space than can be given here. All one can do is to assert, without fear of contradiction, that the child of to-day is happy in his school environment, that he is willing and eager to go to school and that, both physically and spiritually, there is bestowed in turn an amount of care and attention to which his forerunner could lay no sort of claim.

Moreover, it is fair to say, without dispraise of Scottish teachers in earlier years, that children nowadays are taught by men and women better educated, better trained for their tasks than ever before in the country's history. All males entering the profession of teaching in Scotland must be university graduates except in the cases of such specialist subjects as Music, Educational Handwork and Physical Education. While graduation is not absolutely essential for women teachers, the very large proportion do, in fact, take a university degree either as a prelude to, or as an accompaniment of, their professional training as teachers. There are, in fact, few countries in which the prevailing educational standard of the teaching profession is as high as it is in Scotland.

The structure of Scottish education is simple. It proceeds from the Nursery School to the Infants' Department and thence to the two divisions, Primary and Secondary, the break between the two occurring when the average pupil reaches the age of eleven or twelve years. The Nursery School movement is now developing fairly rapidly in the large cities and splendid work is being done for the pre-school child. At about age five or thereby the Infants' Department proper begins. It forms one of the most delightful features of Scottish school life to-day, the children being taught under cheerful conditions by a keen and enthusiastic body of women. In the Primary School emphasis is rightly laid on the groundwork of knowledge in reading, writing, composition, arithmetic, history, geography, drawing and music. Here the pupil begins to show his prowess, and at about eleven is tested in a variety of ways to find whether he is fitted for advancement to the Secondary Division.

In discussing the Secondary School it has to be remembered that the bulk of the children leave school at the statutory leaving age which, from 1939, will be fifteen years. It is highly important, therefore, that they should have a form and content of secondary education which, while not vocational in any strict sense, should be capable of leading on to the work which they may, on leaving school, be able to get. The best curriculum for such pupils is, and always must be, a matter for debate but, substantially, it must proceed on the basis of English, History and Geography, with such additions as Educational Handwork, Domestic Science, Elementary Mathematics, Music and Art. The bias of such a curriculum need not always be the same. Children from a rural school will find an interest and outlet in studies which would be foreign to the mind of the city child. The main object to be achieved is the stimulation of the mind, so that the pupil may end his formal school-days alert and eager to prepare himself, by

135

diverse means and through varying interests and activities, for full citizenship in a democratic state.

For the relatively few who proceed to the full Secondary course, lasting approximately five years, there are to-day in Scotland admirably staffed and equipped schools where ample preparation is afforded for entrance to the University, the Technical Colleges, and to those professions which require the Leaving Certificate of the Scottish Education Department, or its equivalent, as an essential preliminary. The development of these Secondary courses is one of the most remarkable features in Scottish education. In the middle of the nineteenth century the Universities were frequently called upon to perform what is now done universally in the schools themselves, and the rise in the standards of University education is directly attributable to the teaching which boys and girls now get in Classics, Mathematics, Modern Languages and Science at the hands of men and women, the majority of whom hold Honours degrees of the Universities.

It is within the powers of the Education Authorities to grant bursaries to pupils in pursuance of their secondary school and university studies and, while the sums awarded are not perhaps as large as those given to selected pupils south of the Border, they are, nevertheless, of the greatest benefit, particularly when it is recalled that, in the cases of pupils the means of whose parents are inadequate, these bursaries can be supplemented by grants from the Carnegie Trust for the Universities of Scotland.

That, then, is the structure of school education in Scotland from the Nursery School to the highest forms of the Secondary School. But beyond the school there lies a large field of further activity. For the pupil bent on improving himself after his school-days are over, there are the Continuation Classes which are under the care of each Local Authority. Higher in the scale are the finely equipped Technical Colleges, such as the Royal Technical College at Glasgow and the Heriot-Watt College in Edinburgh, and, in the sphere of Commerce, excellently equipped colleges in the main cities. Adult education has made decided advances since the War and, by the recent action of the Marquess of Lothian in gifting Newbattle Abbey as a College of Adult Education, there is now at hand an almost unique opportunity of advanced study for those who, in earlier years, were unable to get any form of higher education.

To crown the edifice, there are the four Scottish Universities, the oldest of which has borne the storm and stress of over five centuries.

In reference to the Universities, I would ask any reader of this article to take down the Calendar of any of the Universities for, say, 1860 and to compare it with the Calendar for the current session. There he will find that in buildings, in staff, in resource of teaching power, in opportunity for research, in amplitude of span and scope, the Universities of Scotland have undergone truly prodigious developments. But — the *laudator temporis acti* may ask me—despite your fine buildings, your halls of residence for students, your large staffs, your manifold courses in Arts, Divinity, Science, Medicine, Engineering, Commerce, are the Universities doing any better work than they did in the quiet years of, say, the nineteenth century? To that there can be no precise and simple answer. If one begins to select individual subjects any sweeping statement becomes impossible. The standard of classics, for example, to-day is not, in my belief, any higher than it previously was. But, on the other hand, the study of the subjects of the medical curriculum, the scope of the physical and natural sciences, the attainments in modern languages—all these, to name only a few examples, have increased in a very marked degree.

The plain truth is that the Universities have marched with the times. The ancient quietude and repose may have gone : the life of the University professor is no longer a leisurely affair : the students present less striking characteristics, perhaps, and seem to emerge more and more from the same mould. But anyone who, because of the modern system of bursaries from Local Authorities and subventions from the Carnegie Trust, is tempted to look upon these ancient institutions as now mainly factories for the turning out of preachers, doctors, lawyers, teachers and engineers, and to regard them as places where less fine work is being done than was the case in earlier times, is going perilously wide of the mark. It is true that the Universities have great problems to face in an endeavour to ensure for the student the benefit of those activities outside of the class-rooms which are so pervasive in their influence and mean so much for the character of the individual undergraduate. The significant thing is that they are active in these problems. If they were not, then indeed they might be held up to reproach as being remote from the needs of the modern world. They suffer considerable monetary disability and are, on the whole, less happily placed in this respect than some of the modern Universities in the great English cities. Yet their innate strength is undiminished. In spirit they are Scottish. They remain true to that tradition by which young men and women, of slender financial resources but high ambition, are enabled to reach out to careers not easily accessible in other countries ; and the tale is not yet finished of those who, from the humblest beginnings, rise, through and by means of their University careers and opportunities, to positions of honour and responsibility in many walks of life.

by
ONE OF THEM

The educational system, however, has called out a certain amount of criticism ; and there are some, like the writer of the following notes, who consider that the results are a little less perfect than the system

THE FRUITS OF THE SYSTEM

I HAVE read Dr Peddie's article and admired it very much. What a beautiful system this Scottish system of education is, I said to myself. From the Nursery School to the Kindergarten, from the Kindergarten to the Elementary, from the Elementary to the Secondary, from the Secondary to the University, the child passes up the ladder of culture by easy stages. Even granted that in many towns and nearly all country districts the first step of that ladder (the Nursery School) is missing as yet, once the child has made the first tremendous adjustment (from home to school) at the age of five, the next twenty years are spent in a miracle of rationalisation. One can almost see the children, rude, uncouth little savages, taken into the process at two, or five, and gradually polished by the loving care of that devoted band of teachers, until they emerge into the labour market as well-disciplined little wage-earners of fifteen ; or bright young clerks of eighteen ; or, ultimate perfection, the university graduates ready to make theses about the ablative absolute with a grant from the Carnegie Trust. If a perfect system can have perfect results, surely this one must be producing the ideal citizens of a civilised state. But is it ?

I have no doubt at all that Scottish education has been planned with admirable intentions. Faced with

140

the social duty of giving every child a start in life, the experts who drew up the code did try to suit that code to the curious sort of life in which the child would find itself: and, just as the rigours of a competitive society have been softened by some humanitarian ideas, the educationalists have tempered the austerities of their code with some humane ideals.

It is true that the better schools are no longer the places of torture they were even twenty years ago, when I was a child. Learning then was indeed a fearful discipline. We were lively children who had been accustomed to a life of great activity, varied with times of complete rest, the natural life of all young growing things. But when we went to school we had to observe a rigid discipline that might not have been out of place in a convict prison. Absolute silence seemed to be the first principle of education then. Absolute silence, unquestioning obedience, concentration on things we did not understand, and then punishment——

There are people—fine fat grown-up people, hearty common-sense men of the kind that get on to education committees—who make grand jokes about the Tawse. Have you ever seen one of them with a red face, a squabby nose and a loud voice saying, "If it hadn't been for the sense that was walloped into me with the tawse, I wouldn't be where I am to-day," implying that he has got about as far as anyone should want to, and that what was good enough for him is good enough for anybody? At such a time you might think of King Tawse as a jolly despot who made geniuses by teaching them how to take pain.

I myself have seen different things: a teacher, maddened by the stale air of the school, the monotony of her life and the hopelessness of keeping 40 children in order, who raved like a lunatic, hit children round the ears, banged them on the heads with their slates and thrashed them until the more sensitive ones were in abject terror and the rest in a state of intense excitement. I myself, an intelligent child and willing to learn, a child for whom knowledge and imagination were delightful adventures, have gone to school for weeks on end, terrified at what might happen if one of our teachers, over-driven to the point of neurosis, were to break out that morning. That is twenty years ago ; but I still waken up afraid, dreaming that I am in the infant room and that my teacher is enjoying a half hour's sarcasm enforced with the tawse on a class of an average age of nine.

There, then, is a good mark for Scottish education to-day : King Tawse has had his liberties a little circumscribed. In theory at least, corporal punishment, as they call it, is regarded as the last resort ; in practice, of course, a lot depends on the teacher's idea of when the last resort is necessary. Some reach the end of their humane resources sooner than others, and one still hears too often of schoolmasters who believe that the fear of the tawse is the beginning of wisdom. But I see signs, with gratitude and envy, that schools are more pleasant places than they were even twenty years ago. The discipline is less ferocious and perhaps more effectual. There are not so many children who go there in fear. Indeed I am often amazed to find that children enjoy going to school. That alone seems like a major revolution in these twenty years.

There are other signs of the humaner education. The best modern school buildings are a tremendous improvement on the older ones. Light, air and colour have been admitted to the rooms. Sometimes there are even baths. The idea has got around that minds work better in pleasant surroundings, that green grass and bright paint may be as stimulating as fear. That is a blessed idea : one that all parents, all responsible people, should encourage. It needs encouragement. There is nothing easier than to think because we have a few such schools everything is perfect in Scottish education. You don't have to look far before you realise that there are a hundred bad old-fashioned schools for every good new one.

That is on the credit side of Scottish education. What is on the other ? Well, a system must be judged by its fruits : and the fruits of the Scottish system are just a little less splendid than they might be.

Look at them this way. A child is a creature with a great deal of curiosity. If you watch a child you will notice that it plays with the utmost seriousness. Suppose it has a board with some holes and a few pegs to fit these holes, it will spend hours, days, fitting the pegs into the holes. Is it just passing the time? Hardly that ! Looking on you would think by its expression that it was trying to understand the mystery of one thing that fitted into another.

So, as it grows older, it has a growing curiosity as to how things work. It works at learning. Here is an example : suppose a grown-up person, a kind uncle maybe, gives a child an elaborate mechanical donkey, he expects the child to be amused by that toy as a going concern. He expects that the child will wind it up and watch the head and tail move, and will go on winding and admiring till next Christmas. But the child is a serious being. If he is interested in the head and tail that go round, he soon wants to know why. After three days admiring he will have two days intolerable curiosity, then a most exciting dissection. What is the result? When the child has taken the mechanical donkey to pieces he may have learned a great deal about the workings of things, about the wonders of machinery, about the ingenuities of science. But he may also have offended his rich uncle with the sight of a hopelessly dismembered toy. The uncle intended the toy for amusement : it was something frivolous to make the child laugh. But the toy was serious to the child. It was something to learn on. It was another step in his work of learning about the world. For life is a serious business to the child, and most delightful when most serious.

During their first five years children are a plague to everyone because they always want to be finding out. That we admit to be a good thing, because all progress has been won by the restless inquiring minds of men. And you'd think we would try to arrange a system of education that would stimulate and methodise those inquiring minds, so that children left school still intensely curious about the world they live in, so that they would never take anything on trust, so that they would always be wanting to know how the wheels go round (specially the wheels within wheels that are so very important everywhere). Well now, does our education produce that sort of children? In spite of all improvements, I am sorry to say that it does not. At least I do not meet those highly desirable products : nor is their influence very noticeable in public life, yet.

Most people will admit, after a bit of thought, that the things they learned best were the things they learned for themselves, because they wanted to know. Now the children go to school wanting to know. Why, then, is it so very hard to teach them there? And why do they leave school knowing so little? How many thousands

of children go to school full of curiosities about everything, and after five years have little curiosity left about
anything? Or, why is it that children so hard to teach
in school are so easy to teach outside, about football,
and motor-cars and gas engines? There can be only
one reason, that the schools are still teaching the wrong
things in the wrong way ; that they are still trying to
make children interested against their inclination,
instead of leading them on through the things about
which they are curious.

We are still trying to teach children to read, so that
they may be able to understand gas engines. It might
pay us better to let the children get enthusiastic about
gas engines first, because they'll very soon *want* to read
about the scientific principles. Once they have the
desire to read they will learn to read in the shortest
possible time. That's a fact. I knew a man to whom
no one was able to teach German as a schoolboy, yet he
learned enough in a year so that he could read German
text-books when a student. Why? Because the learning
of German had a purpose by then.

The elementary school system is much more humane
than it was thirty years ago, but the teaching is still
made tragically ineffective, because the methods do not
encourage the natural curiosity of the children. That
is not the fault of the teachers : they do their best as
long as they have any hope left in them. It is the fault
of a system that expects children to be taught a set
curriculum and to attain a certain standard of proficiency
by stated times.

A teacher is given 30 or 40 children who have
different natures, different interests, different curiosities.
She is expected to teach them geography, spelling,
writing, arithmetic, drawing, nature knowledge, and

goodness knows what else. She must have them all at a certain standard of proficiency by the end of the year, else she will be thought a bad teacher. What can she do? Well, she cannot allow each child to develop through its own interests : in fact she has not time to find out what these interests are. She can only set lessons and try to force as much knowledge into the children as their strength and her weakness will allow. The strain on any teacher with imagination must be dreadful. So is the dulling effect on the children. Curiosity soon dies in the atmosphere of countings and spellings. Children leave school lazy acceptors instead of active explorers. Surely a waste of time and money and potential talents.

I think the parents are to blame. They send their children to school so that they will get an education that will fit them out for a start in the world. The parents know how difficult it is to get that start, and how precarious to maintain, and they do not want to take any risks with their children. Now they see that the schools do give children a kind of education that allows them to make a living (inevitable, since all schools are much about the same) ; they conclude that education is good enough to go on with ; and they are opposed to any change in case it might handicap their children.

That is a pity. It is a very great handicap to the progressive teachers who realise that we might teach more if we tried to teach less. In fact the ideals of the educationalists and the caution of the parents, acting together, have had a very deplorable effect from the point of view of both. For, recognising that children want more practical work, so that they can teach themselves, the Department has introduced practical work into schools. But, keeping an eye on parents of potential clerks, they have not been able to scrap the academic study of the three R's, and geography and Bible. Thus the children cannot concentrate on the handwork and the teachers cannot give the old-fashioned thorough " grounding " in the three R's. The curriculum, the children and the teachers are overloaded ; that is hardly the perfect condition for healthy growth.

I have a great deal of sympathy with Dr Peddie, though he perhaps may not want it. He has outlined a beautiful system, but I suspect that he must sometimes feel the system does not get a chance to do its best. The fears of parents ; the indifference of the general public ; the ignorance of local councillors, elected for almost any reason except an understanding of education— these would make the best of systems less than effective.

There are many more things I would like to write about after reading Dr Peddie's article, but I must restrain myself, and mention only what seems the chief fault of Scottish education—that it still has an academic bias. It will take a long time to get rid of the idea that every school is a gate to the university—a disastrous idea now that education has become universal. (To say, as I do, that every child should have a chance of university education, is not the same as to say that every child should be taught as if it were going there.) Even now, when central schools offer a different exit from a school career, the academic idea persists. That seems a pity.

Take just one instance. What is the most important qualification for an elementary teacher ? Sympathy for and understanding of children. Given these, the amount of academic knowledge needed is very small. Yet teachers in training spend a lot of time on a multiplicity of academic subjects. Graduates spend three years at a university and only one in training college, and even in training college the work is largely academic. Is it not just a little foolish that we make them learn one of the most difficult jobs in the world on classes of 40, that we let them learn on the most delicate material, human minds, which, once flawed, can never be as good again?

It is a beautiful system on paper, but in practice it has not yet solved the problem of giving real education to every child in Scotland. Can it? We must try to make it. The first necessity is a real constructive interest by everyone. Its greatest enemies are the man who says that what was good enough for him is good enough for the rest : and the other who says complacently that Scottish education is the best in the world. Both are wrong.

ARTS AND ARTISTS

A GUIDE TO AMUSEMENT

by
WILLIAM POWER

Perhaps you may wish a guide to books about Scotland, telling who wrote them and why they were written so. Here, then, is a rapid survey that may help you to what you want, either ancient or modern

THEY WROTE ABOUT SCOTLAND

THERE are only two ways of getting to know a country. One is to live in it; the other is to study its literature. The latter plan might lead to misconceptions. For eight of its fourteen centuries of history, Scotland was almost entirely a Gaelic-speaking country, and it has been producing Gaelic literature down to our own day. A foreign student who confined himself to Scots-Gaelic literature would be struck by its exiguity, but he would hardly be prepared to learn that the number of Gaelic speakers in Scotland had shrunk to one-thirtieth of the population.

If the student went on to literature in what by about 1400 had become the dominant Lowland tongue, but did not pursue his studies later than the time of Sir David Lyndsay, the last of the great line of the " makars," he would visualise a Scotland in which the average Scot of to-day would be as little at home as in Portugal. The Scotland reflected in the poetry of Barbour, Blind Harry, Henryson, Kennedy, Dunbar, and Gavin Douglas, and in the prose of Bellenden and Pitscottie, is a Roman Catholic Scotland (less Roman than Catholic), unconscious of the approaching shadow of Knox. Its " wretched poverty " is exemplified by the number and the fine condition of its fighting men,

151

drawn straight from the farm and the smiddy ; by the founding of three Universities, the Continental tours of scholars, the growth of a Navy, the development of trade with France, the Low Countries and the Baltic, the building of royal palaces, country castles and town mansions, and the existence of a greater number of fine cathedrals and abbeys than were to be found in any other northern region of equal size except Flanders.

The monarchs were cultured cosmopolitans, easy-going in their morals, but patriotically zealous for the all-round prestige of Scotland and the welfare of its common folk. They were martyred by their disloyal nobles. But the well-farmed lands of the Kirk gave a steady supply of food, and English invasions and the fights of king and nobles did less damage than the religious wars of the seventeenth century, when Scotland was to experience real poverty.

There had been an early so-called " Scots " series of poems, largely of Arthurian inspiration, and vaguely associated with shadowy personages like Huchown of the Awle Reale and Thomas Rymour of Ercildoune ; but they are really Northern English. In the North-East there grew up a native Teutonic tongue, " Ynglis " in form, but largely Scandinavian in texture. This was Early Scots, the language of Barbour and Wyntoun. In the fifteenth century it developed into Middle Scots, the language of the makars, who, though paying tribute to Chaucer, differed from him in speech. Middle Scots is a mainly poetic language of a unique kind, copious and resonant, richly rhymed, and varying, in its greatest writer, Dunbar, from the aureate stateliness of " The Thrissil and the Rois " to the rollicking lilt of " Kynd Kyttok." Its metrical and thematic range was wider than that of contemporary English. Its poets essayed every known European measure, and combined Latinised terms with the savoury parlance of the farm and the street.

The makars were " art " poets, dealing little in popular forms like the song and the ballad. But it is improbable that knowledge of their works was confined to " clerks " and courtiers. The Scots commonalty have always been active-minded, and until industrialism completed the work done by the theocrats, they had a sense of poetry. The chief traits of the makars are enduringly Scottish : love of nature, colour, and animals ; delight in vivid diction ; satiric humour, seldom unkindly, but occasionally Rabelaisian ; and a proneness to solemn moralising, particularly about death. They do not display the English disdain for the " mob." Scotland had the Celtic tradition of social solidarity. Barbour and Blind Harry are poets of freedom.

Prose and verse in Middle Scots were produced till within the Reformation period. But the old tongue had lost its verve and stateliness. It was fading, on the one hand, into common English, and declining, on the other, into the vernacular that is Modern Scots, a speech that suffers from the confusion of its dialects and the failure of its poets to raise it to the height of " great argument." Ninian Winyet, Knox's Catholic opponent, wrote in Middle Scots, and reviled Knox for attempting to " knap suddrone." Unlike his friend Buchanan, Knox had little interest in Scotland's past. Its literary tongue was associated with the scheme of things he sought to destroy. His soul went marching on. By the second decade of the seventeenth century, the old Scotland had suffered a black-out, and the lineaments of the new Scotland are visible : the Shorter Catechism, the minister, the kirk session, and the Scottish Sabbath.

> Away wes sons off ale and brede,
>   Off wyne and wax, off gamyn and glé . . .

and, though the Scottish Reformation was a necessary assertion of national freedom in spiritual matters, and was to have valuable intellectual results when freedom was better defined, " our gold wes changyd in to lede " so far as Scots literature in the seventeenth century was concerned. Compare Zachary Boyd with Dunbar ! The only poets of real account in the era between the fade-out of Middle Scots and the vernacular revival are Drummond of Hawthornden and the Marquis of Montrose, the one a belated Spenser, the other a Cavalier lyrist of the school of Lovelace. In prose, there is little except the dronings and ravings of the Poundtexts, though in the welter of controversy and dithyramb a Scottish prose style was being formed. Its one outstanding exemplar was a strong Royalist, Sir Thomas Urquhart, whose translation of Rabelais has the verve and gusto of an original work of genius.

Urquhart's superb achievement shows how useful an intimate knowledge of the vernacular may be to a Scots prose-writer. English literature just after his day became arid and anæmic for lack of poetic impulse and elemental inspiration. In Scotland there was a strong subterranean stream of popular poetry, Fescennine, lyrical, and ballad. It began to come to the surface in the vernacular poems of the Sempills. When religious peace was restored, the vernacular revival declared itself in the poems of Lady Grizel Baillie, Lady Elizabeth Wardlaw, and Allan Ramsay, less notable as poet than as anthologist. Ramsay threw a bridge back over the literary gap that Knox had created. In his Doric poems, Fergusson revived the artistry of the old makars and created the moulds for Burns.

The 'Forty-five reawoke interest in things Celtic, and Macpherson mystified Europe with his " Ossian." Scots history was restudied, the ballads were collected, and the way was opened for the fairy poems of Hogg and for the Waverley Novels, which changed the course of world fiction. Smollett had vitalised the picaresque novel. Galt initiated what was to be known as the " Kailyard " school of fiction.

There were also the Scots philosophers : Hutcheson, Hume, Reid, Dugald Stewart. Hume is one of the pivot-men in world thought. Adam Smith expounded the economic system on which the world was to be run for a century-and-a-half. From the " Modern Athens " came germinative ideas on history, æsthetics, and literary criticism, and Edinburgh was to be famous for her " Scotch Reviewers," vivaciously and elaborately misleading. Books like " Jupiter " Carlyle's *Memoirs*, Cockburn's *Memorials*, and Grey Graham's *Social Life of Scotland in the Eighteenth Century*, give some of the reasons why Scotland, having gone so far, did not go farther ; why she never went beyond the retrospective phase of the Romantic Revival ; why writers like Scott, Lockhart, and Wilson were so hopelessly reactionary ; and why Scots literature virtually collapsed soon after the death of Scott.

The Union had deprived Scotland of a real national focus, and of the means of giving national effect to creative ideas. The only national body was the Kirk, which was obscurantist and rather un-Scottish. Politically, Scotland was a mere satrapy. She was driven back upon her past, and her ablest writers became minions of the English Tory Government and bravos of pious Scots landlords who hated the ideas of the French Revolution even more than they hated Napoleon. It was small wonder that Scotland succumbed to the worst influences of industrialism, aggravated by an illiberal evangelicanism, or that most of her brightest spirits took advantage of improved transport to depart for regions where they could not only earn more money but have a freer and more interesting life. Scotland in the first half of last century was an insanitary prison for many of its inhabitants. For " exiles " like Carlyle it was a sanctuary of the more disagreeable virtues.

Failing to note that Burns and Hogg had closed an epoch, the vernacular bards feebly echoed their least characteristic strains. The poets in English imitated, not unskilfully, prevalent English and French styles. Edinburgh had a literary after-glow, in which the chief figure was Aytoun, a Tory romantic in the Lockhart tradition, but more perfervidly Scottish. Scott and the German ballads were the models for his rhetorical *Lays of the Scottish Cavaliers.* He wrote the cleverest skit of his time, *The Massacre of the Macphersons.* The most memorable Scottish books of the period are Hugh Miller's *My Schools and Schoolmasters*, Dr John Brown's *Horæ Subsecivæ*, and Alexander Smith's *A Summer in Skye.* Mrs Oliphant and Dr George Macdonald are far from negligible as novelists, but their works do not form a proportionate balance to English mid-Victorian fiction.

With the loss of national consciousness, Scottish literature was fast perishing. The first law of nature manifested itself in Skene's *Celtic Scotland*, the Highland novels of William Black, and the Scottish studies of

Andrew Lang and Robert Louis Stevenson. Early holidays at Bridge of Allan, near the old centre of Jacobite intrigue, set Stevenson on a track that was to lead farther than he dreamt. He showed Scotsmen that books of superlative literary quality could still be written entirely about Scotland. He revived their interest in the quaint or romantic figures of later Scottish history. By making topography entrancingly alive, he restored their vital contact with their own country.

The process was continued by Crockett for Galloway and by Neil Munro for most of the Highlands. Munro's achievement was the most notable, inasmuch as in a beautiful English transparent to Gaelic idiom he subtly portrayed every type of Highland character in its relation to the natural setting. The " Kailyard," represented mainly by Ian Maclaren and the earlier Barrie, is an interesting irrelevance ; its over-idyllicism moved George Douglas Brown to write *The House with the Green Shutters*, now a classic.

Among Scots poets associated with the English movement in the 'nineties were Lord Alfred Douglas, a master of the sonnet ; and John Davidson, who while in Scotland had written a drama on Bruce. Davidson was the most distinguished Scots poet since Burns. Stevenson had set a new standard in vernacular verse, and he was followed by poets like Logie Robertson, Wingate, and Hendry.

By the time of the War, the stage was set for a general revival of Scots literature. It began with C. M. Grieve's anthologies, *Northern Numbers*, including poems in Doric and English by Lewis Spence, John Buchan, Violet Jacob, Marion Angus, Alexander Gray, William Jeffrey, William Soutar, and other writers. Their work, particularly that of Spence, Jeffrey, and Soutar, showed a remarkable advance in thought and technique beyond anything produced in Scotland in pre-War days. The movement was to be notably reinforced by poets like Edwin Muir and William Montgomerie ; and Robert Bain wrote a fine verse-drama, successfully performed and broadcast, on *James I. of Scotland*. The most vital figure in the movement was Grieve himself (" Hugh MacDiarmid "), the Tyrtæus of modern Scotland, whose poetic range, mostly in " Synthetic Scots," extends from exquisite lyrics to long verse-sequences in which affairs of Scotland are vividly treated in a world perspective. The plays of " James Bridie " have also a foremost place in modern Scots literature.

Outstanding books in Scots history and biography are those of Law Mathieson, D. A. Mackenzie, Evan Barron, Dr G. P. Insh, Professor Dewar Gibb, George Malcolm Thomson, Miss I. F. Grant, Dr A. O. Anderson, Agnes Mure Mackenzie, Dr W. Mackay Mackenzie, James W. Fergusson ; the studies of Montrose by John Buchan (Lord Tweedsmuir) and Margaret Irwin, Catherine Carswell's *Burns*, and Donald Carswell's *Brother Scots*. The translation work of Edwin and Willa Muir is in the high tradition of Charles Scott-Moncrieff. First-rate descriptive books on Scotland or Scottish districts have been written by J. J. Bell (author of *Wee MacGreegor*), George Blake, George Scott-Moncrieff, and other writers. A book that is in a class by itself is Moray M'Laren's *Return to Scotland*. Unique, also, are the delightful farming sketches of John R. Allan.

The dominant figure in Scots literature in our time was the late R. B. Cunninghame Graham, the perfect type of the Scots cosmopolitan. Though Scotland figures little in his biography, he knew it well, and many of his best stories and sketches are on Scots themes. His poignantly ironic realism undoubtedly influenced the change in Scots fiction that took place after the War. One of the first novelists to depart from the sentimental and rather Sundayfied optimism of the older school was George Blake, best known by *The Shipbuilders* ; but James Bryce, in *The Ploughboy*, had done likewise. Graphically true pictures of Highland life are given by Ian Macpherson in *Land of our Fathers*, and by Neil Gunn in *Butcher's Broom* and *Highland River*. *Men of Ness* is a vivid reconstitution of old Norse life in Orkney by the author of *Juan in America*. Robert Craig's *Traitor's Gate* is a striking piece of historic realism. Christine Orr's *Gentle Eagle* brings James IV. fully alive. Edinburgh is the scene of Bruce Marshall's brilliant fantasy, *Father Malachy's Miracle*.

James Barke's *Major Operation* is a powerful indictment of social conditions in the industrial West. Poetry, grim realism, biting irony, and whimsical humour, racy of the soil of his native Kincardineshire, are inimitably blended in the *Sunset Song* and *Cloud Howe* of Lewis Grassic Gibbon, whose early death deprived Scotland of one of the most brilliant of her sons.

Among regional novelists mostly in the older tradition are Agnes Mure Mackenzie in the Highlands, Nan Shepherd in Aberdeenshire, Edward Albert in Edinburgh, and, in the West, Dot Allan, Lennox Kerr, George Woden, Nancy Brysson Morrison, and, among the finest of all, Frederick Niven. John Buchan's romances and the Highland novels of L. A. G. Strong and Maurice Walsh, both Irishmen, are well known. Few but precious are the pages devoted to Scots life by that great literary artist, Compton Mackenzie, who collaborated with John Lorne Campbell in *The Book of Barra*.

If Scots poetry hardly seems to have fulfilled the promise of the first few years after the War, the reason is mainly the difficulty of publishing. The cessation of *The Modern Scot*, which gave hospitality to verse and prose of a pioneer character, was a calamity, and Scotland is in need of a literary and critical magazine of an advanced type. In history and biography there has been real progress. The old ultra-Protestant and anti-Celtic prejudices have been overcome, social and economic history is being given its due place, and, for the first time, we are beholding Scotland's past as it really was. The revaluations of Burns and Scott have increased our real appreciation of these writers, and have helped to clear the way for modern literature. Fiction and general literature have definitely improved in quality, and they have become truer to the realities of life. From Scots literature of last century, it is almost impossible to obtain a clear and reliable picture of Scots life at that time. But the Scotland of the post-War years is faithfully and graphically mirrored in contemporary Scots literature. That of itself constitutes a real " literary renaissance."

SOME BOOKS ABOUT SCOTLAND

A Short History of Scotland. George Malcolm Thomson.
Scotland : The Ancient Kingdom. Donald A. Mackenzie.
The Scottish War of Independence. Evan M. Barron.
The Highlands and Isles of Scotland. W. C. Mackenzie.
Studies in Scots History, Reformation to 1843. W. Law Mathieson.
Domestic Annals of Scotland. Dr Robert Chambers.
Criminological Studies. William Roughead.
Social Life of Scotland in the Eighteenth Century. Grey Graham.
Memoirs of Alexander Carlyle.
Cockburn's *Memorials.*
Early Travellers in Scotland. Hume Brown.

Journeys in Scotland.   Defoe.
Western Islands of Scotland.   Martin Martin.
Wade in Scotland.   J. B. Salmond.
Journal of a Tour in the Hebrides.   Boswell.
Tours in Scotland.   Pennant.
A Summer in Skye.   Alexander Smith.
Robert Louis Stevenson and the Scottish Highlanders.   David B. Morris.
The Entail.   John Galt.
Memoirs of a Justified Sinner.   James Hogg.
The Scenery of Scotland.   Sir Archibald Geikie.
Scotland and the Scots.   William Power.
The Heart of Scotland.   George Blake.
Galloway.   C. H. Dick.
Return to Scotland.   Moray M'Laren.
Scottish Country.   Edited by G. Scott-Moncrieff.
Scottish Journey.   Edwin Muir.
Historical Survey of Scottish Literature.   Agnes Mure Mackenzie.
The Life of Robert Burns.   Catherine Carswell.
Celtic Literature.   Magnus Maclean.
The Road to the Isles.   Kenneth Macleod.
The Northern Muse.   Edited by John Buchan.
Holyrood.   Edited by W. H. Hamilton.
The Scots Week-end.   Catherine and Donald Carswell.
The Scots Book.   Compiled by Ronald MacDonald Douglas.
The Book of Scottish Ballads.   Blackie & Son.
To Circumjack Cencrastus and *Stony Limits.*   Hugh MacDiarmid.
Fantasia in an Industrial Town.   William Jeffrey.
Nursery Rhymes.   William Soutar.
Books on the Highlands and Hebrides, by Seton Gordon, Alasdair
    Alpin MacGregor, Iain F. Anderson, Ratcliffe Barnett, Hugh
    Quigley, Thomas Hannan, and others.
Bound volumes of *The Modern Scot.*

About the best books to consult, if one has time,
are county and local histories, volumes of extracts from
Sheriff Court records, family and other memoirs and
papers, and books of the type of Crawford's *Renfrewshire.*

If there is not a great deal of creation in these arts there is at least considerable activity. Here a critic is rather critical about what we have to offer as recreation for a civilised gentleman

THEATRES, MUSIC AND PAINTING

CAN Scotland entertain you in its own way? Yes! If you come to the right places, at the right times.

Glasgow is the centre of the Pantomime Universe — and its Pantomime is predominantly Scots. This winter, Scots comedians lavished Aberdeen jokes, Glesca humour and Scots daftness on the audiences in the Alhambra, the Theatre Royal and the Princess's Theatre. For four hours at a time, and from a week before Christmas until the beginning of summer, the Princess's Theatre has been producing pawky pantomimes ever since tartan was invented, or thereabouts. They just escape being all-the-year-round entertainments. A Town Councillor who had attended well over half a century of Princess's first nights was elevated to the Lord Provostship, and then Knighted. George West is the reigning comedian.

Glasgow can support eight or more pantomimes at a time. And it does. Edinburgh's taste in pantomimes runs to the faded gentility of the Scots dames of the late Tommy Lorne. Glasgow goes West.

For five years Glasgow and Edinburgh have loyally allowed a Repertory Company to amuse them at reduced prices. Audiences have used their season tickets regularly for three-quarters of the year, including the summer months, while the company played nice, well - established comedies by Barrie, Lonsdale, Coward, Maugham, Shaw and anybody else who didn't exceed the speed limit of the intelligence of the tired business man, or his typist and her boy friend. Perth and Ayr have the same degree of enthusiasm for their resident Repertory Companies' not too daring sequence of drama.

Other theatres in Glasgow and Edinburgh are the recognised stages for the dress rehearsals of plays and musical comedies on the way to London. These dress rehearsals are billed as " World Première." But the bills don't fill the theatres unless the leads are " stars " like Coward, Lawrence, Tempest, Seidl, Howes, Courtneidge or Lupino. Even then you never can tell.

It is difficult to say what London producers learn from a preliminary run in Glasgow or Edinburgh. *Night Must Fall*, which deserved its London success, had a mediocre beginning in Scotland. *The Boy David* failed lamentably in London. In Edinburgh, it crowded the King's Theatre for weeks with dressy and devout worshippers.

Ballet, English or Franco-Russian, has its vicissitudes in these two cities. So has opera. The cheaper parts of the theatres respond. But if it isn't the vogue at the moment in the West End, the stalls are filled with wide-open spaces and dead-heads.

Is there a Scottish drama ? Glasgow has the Scottish National Players. Their early experiments with Scottish or national plays landed them with an unreliable following, as well as one or two playwrights and actors like James Bridie and Eliot Mason. These playwrights and actors were gradually adopted by

London. Now, the Scottish National Players occasionally toy with the revival of a London success. They still have braw guid Scots comediennes among them.

The most enterprising dramatic movement in Scotland is the Curtain Theatre, of Glasgow. It produces comedies, tragedies and historical dramas by Scots playwrights not yet famous.

Scotland is effervescing everywhere with the activities of the amateur actors who figure in Drama Festivals. Only a hero would volunteer to produce a play with so many vain and self-confident amateurs in his company. But though they hate him if he is a disciplinarian, he can count on the box-office support of their sisters, and their cousins and their aunts.

The same goes for the family fans of the big amateur operatic societies in the cities. For a week, while leading ladies with thin voices and thick arms, and gawky juvenile leads with bald heads, and battalions of raw recruits to the "business" of the chorus are lolloping behind the footlights, the auditorium is crowded with relatives whose naïve behaviour betrays their strangeness to the theatre.

Scotland is blissfully content with Hollywood films and the National Government. Consequently there is no spirit of revolt yearning for real life dramas about the under-dog, or about the heroes or villains of the capitalist state. Reality of working-class existence is commonplace to the working-classes. So they are utterly apathetic to any of the very few plays that profess to dramatise them. Propaganda plays fail, because they are not plays, and only the converted listen to them.

Universities and Scotland's other famous educational

institutions do not cultivate an intelligentsia. So far as their instructors and students are aware, drama and literature stopped, when history ended, several decades ago. Their students travel daily by bus to the Universities, feverishly " take down " lectures for degree passes there, and return each afternoon to their villages and towns to swot, and to escape to the fitba' and the cinema. Or they just stay put in their logdings.

How does Scotland entertain itself in the summer months ? In the two cities so often mentioned already, the zero hour for laughter in the theatre is later than in the winter. Variety as a form of revue has built up genial, steady audiences. In resorts like Rothesay, Largs, Aberdeen, Dunoon and Ayr the entertainers have all a Scots comedian. His topical thrusts are far removed from the softness that passes as Scots humour in England. And every entertainers' troupe embraces a tenor or a baritone who brings his sentimental ballads from his experience on more exalted stages.

How does Scotland fare for music ? The Scottish Orchestra and the Orpheus Choir are the biggest musical achievements of the country. And they are big. And they are Clyde-built.

The Scottish Orchestra has its ups and downs. Its conductors have included some of the world's famous musicians—and some of its social successes. Georg Szell, the present conductor, has moulded the Orchestra into a grand instrument. The populace discovered this during the Plebiscite Programme, when it turned up in thousands and usurped the places occupied by the faithful musical public during the previous two or three winter months.

Like the theatres, the Orchestra has to be chary of novelties. Beethoven, Mozart, Wagner, Brahms,

Haydn and even Bach are familiar, and therefore not repulsive. But composers whose works have already become well known to Continental audiences are still " modern " to Scotland. They have to be introduced in homœopathic doses. And it is doubtful if either high-brows or low-brows in Scottish audiences admit or know whether there are any Scottish composers beyond those " Anons " whose tunes inspired Burns's lyrics.

The Orpheus Choir has no downs, only ups. As a result of the ruthless discipline and rigorous training of Sir Hugh Roberton, it is the perfect choir. Its perfection verges on the precious. It does only those part songs and choruses from Scots sources, religious music, the Hebrides or the Classics that it can do perfectly in tone and articulation. Its programme is always as mercilessly in step with the best taste as a row of synchronising dancers. A human *faux pas* by one of these dancers is a relief to people who hate to watch machinery all their lives.

These musical organisms visit other cities and towns in Scotland. The Orpheus Choir is the darling of Royalty and Prime Ministers. Edinburgh has a season of the Scottish Orchestra, and has an Orchestra of its own, as well as a Choir with a reputation. In both cities, the Music departments of the Universities are energetic. And these towns share the concerts of excellent music and of celebrities with the circuit of English provincial cities.

Is that all the music in Scotland? Oh, no! Every town of any size has its amateur orchestra. And then there are the Highland Games, and the Mod and Gaelic Concerts. On these occasions it is advisable to wear a kilt, if you wish to look as if pibrochs, reels and strathspeys filled you with delicious but well-controlled despair for the lost heritage of Caledonia. You may also attend a Ceilidh. But if you have not the Gaelic, it is more than likely that you are a Philistine who does not recognise that the singers are not repeating the same sad lilt all evening, with the same senile, nasal sentimentality.

Scottish restaurants and tea-rooms are mercifully free from the music that insists on accompanying meals in other countries. And there are probably fewer cacophonous dance bands to the square mile than across the Border.

Where can you see paintings? Towns like Kilmarnock, Kirkcaldy and Paisley have permanent collections. They are often housed with the mummies and the model ships in the local museum. Resurrected Victorians would renew acquaintance with old favourites among them. Glasgow's collection is catholic. It contains many masterpieces in a gallery that is a piquant contrast to the architecture of its School of Art. The National Gallery in Edinburgh is stocked with the best traditions of Scottish portraiture and landscape painting. And if you like family albums with life in them, the National Portrait Gallery is the place for you. The bust of Bonnie Prince Charlie there is the epitome of the Stuart Dynasty and all its descendants. Examine it for yourself.

Prices for old masters notwithstanding, the best Scottish artists are not all dead. On the artistic calendar nearly every month is the date for some exhibition which has character. The Society of Scottish Artists distinguishes December by flaunting (fairly) youthful artists, scorning tradition (somewhat) and inviting dancing dervishes from abroad to show Scotland what foreign artists are doing now. In January, the Society of Eight groups some of Lavery's journalistic vivacities alongside the carefully selected works of the other handful of highly individual painters in its membership. The Royal Scottish Water Colour Society decorates February with its versatility in using or disguising its medium. And soon after, the Society of Artist Print Makers demonstrates its tricks with woodcuts, lithographs, etchings, engravings and what not. These are all Edinburgh events.

So is this—at the end of April the military turns out. So do the tall hats of commissionaires, of Society, and of gentlemen artists, and the sombreros of lady artists. They are attired, according to their own conceits, to match the occasion. It is the opening of the Royal Scottish Academy Exhibition. This Exhibition is also guaranteed to match the classic lines of the Academy's Galleries with the pictures on its line.

Glasgow's retort to all this is the Institute. In the Springtime of Art in the West, the famous Glasgow School flourished. The Institute opens in [the Autumn.

Young painters are perhaps too shy to gate-crash among the myriads of pictures from these mellow artists. But occasionally the youngsters hold one-man shows in Glasgow. They have much more to say for their experimental expressions than the dilettantes who supply exhibits to the Exhibitions in smaller towns. But that's not why their pictures are not all sold. They believe it is because the people who have money to buy pictures have the minds of the pre-camera age. Their portraits must not tell them or the world the grim truth about their souls. They don't want actual life and work around them exposed in paint. Their landscapes have

EXPERIMENTAL : Tait's Tower at the Empire Exhibition

EXPERIMENTAL : The Hall of Industry at the Empire Exhibition

TRADITIONAL : Fishworkers at the Kiln in Aberdeen

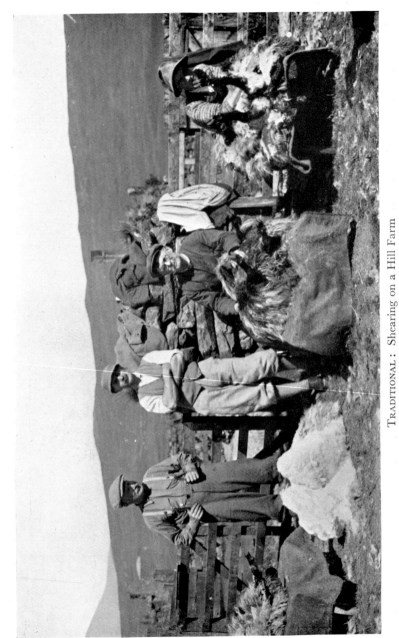

TRADITIONAL : Shearing on a Hill Farm

to be the old sweet songs about the country that is vanishing.

But maybe pictures are not sold just because these people live in motor cars, dine and drink in road-houses, and sleep between walls that cannot stand up to the vigour of young, impertinent art.

by
COLM BROGAN

If there is no Scottish Theatre of any consideration, Scotland does produce some comedians of excellent entertainment. Let us now remember Tommy Lorne and read about the treasures of the Queen's

THE GLASGOW COMEDIANS

IT is really peculiar that Scotland should be, as it certainly is, the home of comedians, for the country is not spontaneously amusing. The climate is cold and wet, ideas in religion tend to be severe, and politics of the most bigoted kind are taken neat in large quantities. " Scotch comedian," of course, is a technical term. The laddies and lassies celebrated by Harry Lauder are as conventional as the Corydons and Phyllises of pastoral poetry. Roamin' in the gloamin' is popular enough on the bonnie banks of Clyde, but not in kilts. The grass is usually wet.

There are sensitive spirits who object to Lauder's kilt and knobbly stick. " Here is a Scot," they say, " deliberately making a farce of the national dress for the benefit of a vulgar and foreign audience in London." But they are unfair to Lauder. He never betrayed his country. He wasn't a Scotchman making a clown of the typical Scotchman, but a Lowlander making a clown of the Highlander, which is quite a traditional thing to do.

Lauder's busiest days are long past. He is no longer young and it is not in the nature of things that his huge popularity should have lasted unimpaired, but he didn't help himself by giving entertainments which partly resembled a prize distribution speech and partly a service of praise. His fondness for giving advice on industrial disputes from the stage did much to make the thought of parting less painful to his former workmates of the Lanarkshire pits. " Sing at your wark," said the gallant Scottish knight. " Keep right on tae the end of the road. Min' Ah'm tellin' you." His work *was* singing, and it never occurred to him that by preaching instead he was lying back on the job. It was a distressing aberration but not at all unnatural. If every great clown wants to play Hamlet, Scotch comedians are apt to fancy themselves as Polonius.

The homilies were exceedingly inartistic. When Simple Sammy put on a grave look and announced that his second name was Smiles, he spoiled the willing suspension of unbelief. Lauder was never much of an actor. Strictly speaking, he wasn't even a comedian but a concert entertainer. His voice was excellent, his songs were nicely judged Burns and water ; he had a really good stage presence and some of his jokes were funny. Also, he was carbolically clean.

The next to Lauder among the conventional or pastoral comics is Will Fyffe. He is what is called a character actor, but his characters are not real. They are conceived in the mood of the Bonnie Brier Bush. Even his famous Glasgow working-man is a patronising fantasy, with no justification in the great truths of historical dialectic as understood in the Spoutmouth and the Gorbals. Will Fyffe is really clever, but it is an undeniable fact that there are more people like Jack Buchanan in Scotland than there are like any of the Will Fyffe characters.

The pastoral comics are all more or less divorced from reality. The other kind, the industrial comics, is nearer the bone. The greatest of these was the still lamented Tommy Lorne. Tommy's real name was Hugh Corcoran. He was bred in one of the most wretched slums in Europe and he knew Glasgow under the skin. The Clyde for him and his like was the stretch of water which separates the mortuary from the Gorbals. His best days as an artist were spent in the Gorbals. It is not a pretty neighbourhood, nor is it oppressively Scotch. Kosher meat is much in demand, and the pubs have names like Rooney. The local colour is Red.

The Princess pantomime begins in December and it stops in early summer. It doesn't go in much for Tiller Girls or transformation scenes, but it does try to be funny. Tommy gave impersonations there that will still be talked of by senile persons in 1990. He was a tram conductor on an all-night car and a continuous dancer with enormous bandages on his feet. He was a very individual Dame. Tommy was tall and angular, and when he was dressed as a woman he was mostly bones and two mournful and apprehensive eyes. His Dame was a weel-daein' working-class woman, with a lot of jerky dignity, determined not to be put on, but finding the world too much for her. She had beautiful squeals of indignation and moments of outraged stillness when she mutely asked Heaven if this or that outrage could be, and only the mobile lips and trembling fingers witnessed to the turmoil within.

Tommy's hands were wonderful. In moments of conscious innocence and triumph, they were folded (in white gloves) on his stomach, where they lay like doves asleep. When suspicion of some indignity entered the Dame's mind they stirred, and when shocks of nervous excitement went through her body, every finger had a separate and hysterical life.

Popularity was Tommy's downfall. He went to the Royal in Glasgow and then to Edinburgh, in among the Tiller Girls and the Grand Finales. But he had marvellous moments up to the end. In his last Glasgow pantomime he sat, as Dame, on a log with a love-lorn maiden. The poor Dame described her romance with a gentleman friend many years ago. With coy giggles and nudges she told how they would go to a field and push over a cow to get a warm place. But Fate took the gentleman friend away. As the Dame began to hint at the sad end, her mouth trembled and her fingers shuddered with woe. At last, her face simply melted. It was very delicately done.

There was nobody quite like Tommy. Glasgow could bear the loss of all her M.P.'s and town councillors with Roman fortitude, but the sudden death of Tommy Lorne was a cause of real public grief. It was sad to think that we would never again hear about the woman who kept the wee pie shop in Limphinan, or watch the tall figure of the Dame standing awkwardly and uncertainly rigid, with occasional subsidences, like a camp chair. Life was the poorer for everybody.

The most successful of the surviving local comedians is Tommy Morgan. Morgan is fat and bouncing and artless looking, but he is really very clever. He is not so subtle as Tommy Lorne was, and he repeats himself too much, but he is perfectly authentic, and he never descends to the pathetic ; he has a mind above such emotional putrefactions. At times he has a happy touch of what for some peculiar reason is called " honest " vulgarity. Unfortunately he is becoming exceedingly popular ; and, unless he is careful and very intelligent, he will begin to make right deviations in his act, and his pure proletarian attractiveness will be diminished.

The stoutest fortress of a grand tradition is not the Princess or even the Metropole, but the Queen's. The Queen's is in Watson Street, behind Glasgow Cross. It is a small theatre without even a bar. Prices are reasonable—fourpence, eightpence and a shilling. The pantomime is a twice-nightly show and its principal comedian is Sam Murray. By instinct and tradition the pantomime is unrefined, and it would be foolish to pretend that Sam Murray does anything at all to raise the general tone. When he comes in as a Green Lady (Corporation visitor) and takes a celluloid baby on his knee, honest vulgarity has the house to itself. Sam Murray is an addition to our national life, but he is not alone. He is supported by a host of able colleagues. " Host " is perhaps an exaggeration, for the Queen's is lined with mirrors which give a rich effect of three pantomimes at once, and what with that and the bar being the nearest pub. outside, it is possible that the number of comedians is really less than it seems. But there are certainly several and they are all good. Next to Sam Murray in distinction is Doris Droy. She is full of life and fire and she is as honest as the day is long. Her voice is wonderfully strong. Her top notes are a punch on the ear. She is never tired.

In fashionable pantomime there is a big discrepancy of mood between the blue-nosed element of the comedians and the romantic element of the principal boy and girl. There is no such weakness about the Queen's. The unity of action is strictly preserved. The pantomime is one solid chunk of Glesga.

But even the Queen's is threatened with danger.

Treachery is unthinkable ; the danger comes from outside. It is impossible to imagine Sam Murray keeping right on to the end of the road or Doris Droy being winsome in the Steamie. But they are in danger of having their audience diluted. Half the enjoyment of a Queen's pantomime is the simple but Aristotelian pleasure of recognition, and it is impossible to guess how much encouragement the performers derive from a perfect community of thought and feeling with the audience. That is in danger of being lost, because the clients of more fashionable houses are beginning to discover the Queen's. The Queen's may become a fad. If it does, Genius and Art will take wing and they will not perish in flight. There are haunts as yet unsuspected by the bourgeois. Somewhere or other, honesty will find a home.

by
WILL Y. DARLING

Some notes on Agreeable Eating in
Scotland by one who is Treasurer of
Edinburgh Corporation, a fashionable
draper and the most distinguished
figure in Princes Street

FOOD IN THESE PARTS

THE phrase, "The wine of the country," is familiarly on the lips—and it might be added, the palates—of all travellers, and Scotland does not lack in appropriate beverages. The Usquebaugh of Scotland is assuredly the world's most unique beverage, for no other beverage is produced within such a limited area to the exclusion of all others.

The wines of France have their kin in Belgium, Germany, Switzerland, Italy and Greece, not to speak of South Africa and Australia; but the native drink of Scotland is so unique that in recent months a daring Canadian producer of the beverage has established himself in Scotland in order that what was formerly, at best, a good imitation, may now become " the real Mackay."

The Scots economist feels very keenly that this unique product of Scottish industry should be made the basis of what is not unfairly described as " Penal Taxation." The Scotsman perhaps is so accustomed to giving generously to the world that he does not feel it as keenly as, for example, the people of Lancashire or Yorkshire would if their native product were made to such a large extent one of the principal elements of national taxation.

This essay is intended to deal principally with

Scottish food, but one cannot divorce, fortunately, food from drink so easily and a word must be said about Scottish beer.

The increasing export business which is done in Scottish beer justifies the claim that it is unequalled in the world. Edinburgh, Glasgow, Falkirk, Alloa—these are four centres where this glorious beverage is brewed.

The narrow days of teetotal agitation are fortunately past, and now one can look upon both these beverages with almost a vegetarian eye. After all, they are vegetable products. They follow in analogy the making of tea—they are immersed in boiling water and the result is a beverage which makes glad the heart of man.

If whisky and beer are Scotland's two leading drinks, milk certainly is entitled to a third place; and Scotland produces, from the finest herds in the world, easily the best milk, despite machinations of the Milk Marketing Boards and similar large scale organisations.

Milk is the basis too of some of Scotland's most famous dishes. Whisky and milk—there has already been enough said about whisky, we will leave it on one side—curds and cream—porridge and milk—and cheese—and butter. The individual qualities of all these Scottish milk products are perhaps not appreciated as highly as they should be by Scotsmen. The present writer knows a Frenchman who journeys once a year to Scotland in order to please his palate with the cheese and butter of Scotland as a contrast to Camembert and Normandy. This distinctiveness we who live in Scotland perhaps do not rate sufficiently highly.

Scottish bread—ordinary baker's bread—has a definite flavour of its own in which the visitor finds a new delight. The traveller in England must have been struck by the occasional sight of a sign above a baker's door, "Scottish Bakery," and this is a tribute to Scottish achievement in this field.

Scottish cakes, scones, pastry, made from Scottish butter and Scottish milk take as high a place in the minds of international epicures as the *pâtisseries* of Brussels or Vienna. No country makes oatcakes and scones as Scotland does, and if a unanimous vote on Scottish food were sought, it would probably be to these that the Scottish epicure would point with the greatest pride.

From the point of view of the tourist, however—and from his point of view rather than that of the Scots themselves—haggis, shortbread, and currant bun make the readiest appeal. They have the merit of convenience, when enclosed in the appropriate tin, of being more portable than the scones, and it is this merit, perhaps, which has tended to make them universally eaten from one Pole to the other and right round the Equator and back again.

It is climate ultimately which determines the kind of food which folk eat.

The Scottish climate makes men hungry, and hungry folk like starchy foods, " filling foods " as they are called —breads and scones and thick soups. Scottish broth is different from and better than any vegetable soup made anywhere. The quality of the vegetables as well as the stock which is its base has everything to do with it. The vegetables grown in the hard, trying and difficult climate of Scotland have a quality almost personal to themselves. You cannot make Scotch broth with English turnips and French onions. The vegetables must be, like the meat and bones which are the basis of the stock, Scottish grown.

The meats of Scotland have commanded the attention of Smithfield, and no higher commendation can come from the Englishman than the tribute of his belly. Scotch beef and Scotch mutton hold pride of place and none approach or challenge them, while Scotch venison and Scotch small game generally always find the first place in the market and the highest place in the opinion of the buyer.

Then there are the fish—the salmon, the trout and the herring, the lobsters and the crabs—all distinctively different and all pre-eminently Scottish.

It will be observed that there is no order in this catalogue of Scottish Food. The items do not follow the bill of fare; they come as nature brings them in season and out of season, always stimulating to the imagination and exciting to the appetite.

But one must begin to put these ideas in some sort of sequence.

Let us begin the day from the visitor's point of view.

Let him call for a glass of hot water wherewith to clean the palate and stimulate the digestion.

The waters of Scotland, whether they be from Strathpeffer, St Ronan's Well, or from the Highland stream, are not as the waters of other lands. Scotsmen may well say, " Are not the rivers of Scotland more than the rivers of Babylon ? "—and if they did say so they would say so in truth.

Begin the day, therefore, my dear visitor to Scotland, with the glass of hot water and proceed an hour later to a noble breakfast commencing with porridge from Scottish oats, milk or cream from Scottish cows, and— if you must sweeten the dish—there are sugars which are made in Scotland, but let me commend to you the golden syrup or treacle of Greenock—a Scottish production of over a hundred years.

From the porridge you will proceed to the finnan haddock or the grilled trout, and then to the Ayrshire bacon, Lanarkshire tomatoes and eggs from the farm over the hill. If you must drink a beverage, they do tea better in Scotland than they do coffee as a rule, and much talent and genius has been put to the task of blending teas—grown by Scotsmen in India and Ceylon —with the waters of the native land—for which in their exile they pine.

You will smoke after your breakfast and do not forget that Scotland has its own tobacco industry, having produced on the Clyde and in Edinburgh better tobaccos long before ever Bristol became the principal centre of that industry.

You may spend the morning as you like, but when you return for your luncheon some Scottish ale or a glass of whisky will make the only *apéritif* that is appropriate to the climate.

Luncheon may consist of Scottish broth, boiled salmon, roast beef—with green peas and new potatoes in season—pastry or tart, followed by a whang of Dunlop or Scottish Cheddar cheese.

You will not want any tea. This is an English meal and you can dispense with it. The ladies of the party will desire it and you should see that they have some scones and tarts and perhaps these " Petticoat Tails " which the romantics tell us are a recipe handed down from Queen Mary's days when they were known as " petit gatelles."

You will scorn the tea, doubtless ; and, striding again across the moors and mountains or charging the bunkers, at seven you will be ready for the evening meal. Let it be worthy of yourself and of the land in which you find yourself.

Having lunched as you have done, an alternative menu must be provided. Smoked salmon as a *hors-d'œuvre* followed by hare soup : you would then have grilled Moray Firth soles and proceed to the roast mutton. You may prefer the loin, but for the grand meal the saddle is indicated, especially if you will support it with that distinctive quality of claret which, imported through Leith, is a different beverage altogether from what one drinks in France.

You will have the red currant jelly and baked potatoes and the appropriate sprouts, cabbage or cauliflower. Your sweet should be a substantial one and your fancy might turn to Scottish trifle made of Scottish sponge cakes, heightened with port or sherry, or you might prefer a couple of good Scotch apples, well baked. In any case, the joys of the table are not over with that course, for a Scottish savoury awaits your further delectation. It might well be a croute of herring or a cheese and bacon savoury, or you might resume again the acquaintance which you made at luncheon with the Scottish Cheddar.

Claret I have commended ; but for this meal too —only if you feel like it—there is the aforementioned whisky, beer, and certainly the liqueur. You might do a great deal worse than sample the well-known Scottish liqueur, Drambuie, made of honey and whisky, in which Prince Charlie himself toasted his fortune in the '45.

The great satisfactions of life are not in the achievements of the League of Nations nor in the balanced budgets of National Governments, nor the revolutionary proposals of reformers. You know, dear reader, that happiness is a smaller thing than these. It consists in a day well spent, and the essential of a day well spent is a day with good digestion, a day in which appetite has been satisfied but not sated. Such is the achievement of Scottish food ; it invokes the appetite and it gives a satisfaction which is among the world's greater contentments.

SATURDAY AFTERNOON

THE GAMES OF THE PEOPLE

Is Association Football a game or a religion? Who are the Old Firm? Why does the Heart of Midlothian suffer from syncope? Are the supporters more than the players of the game? These questions are answered by a by no means disinterested spectator

by
COLM BROGAN

THE LEAGUE AND THE CUP

IN a passage of characteristically sombre eloquence on the re-emergence of the Ulster Problem after the War, Mr Winston Churchill described the floods subsiding and the melancholy steeples of Tyrone and Fermanagh rising again from the sinking waters, much to the annoyance of British politicians who had hoped to be rid of them for ever. Precisely the same feelings of irritation afflicted the bosoms of unattached football enthusiasts when serious competition was renewed after the War and the Old Firm immediately reoccupied their historic positions at the head of the League.

The Old Firm, it need hardly be said, are Celtic and Rangers. Their monopoly and the nature of their rivalry have no parallel in football outside of Scotland. With them, as with the worshippers under the melancholy steeples, the Battle of the Boyne is still a matter of lively dispute and recapitulation. Racial, historical and religious considerations inflame the excitement of the supporters. In fact, a Celtic-Rangers match is as much a contest of supporters as of players. They occupy different ends of the park and shout at each other. The Celtic fans are much given to hymn-singing. The Rangers, being less religious but more politically-minded, encourage their champions by songs which celebrate ancient deeds of battle and massacre. In the good old days when ricketties and bugles, painted steel helmets and banners, added a fine gaiety of sound and colour to the proceedings, the scene was very lively indeed. The violence of the rivalry among the supporters is very remarkable indeed. Sometimes it leads to fights and arrests. It is exceedingly profitable for both clubs.

In post-War years Rangers have won the League championship fourteen times out of eighteen, which is a virtual monopoly. On the other hand, they developed a habit of losing the Scottish Cup so abruptly and unexpectedly that it looked as if they were letting the precious object fall out of their hands. In 1920 they were beaten by a fledgling First Division club after drawing twice, and that was astonishing. Next year, they got into the Final and were most unexpectedly beaten by Partick Thistle. The year after, they were in the Final again with Greenock Morton, a team which would not be considered to have any chance with them in a League match. To make things quite hopeless for Morton, their star player had to call off, and it was said that the management thought so little of the team's chances that they did not bring a single bottle of wine against the possibility of having to fill the Cup. Yet, quite early in the first half the Rangers were bunching together nervously in the field and a supporter on the terracing lifted his bugle and dismally played, " It's all over now." The musical mourner was justified in the event. It is also said (though it sounds too good to be true) that Morton borrowed a couple of bottles from the Rangers to fill their trophy.

Worse was still to come. Rangers drew Celtic in the Semi-Final when Celtic were doing very badly indeed.

It was now obvious that Rangers had the Cup jitters, but they always play best against their old rivals, and the disparity in form was so glaring and well-established that even the usually confident Celts took the field in a very anxious mood. But they beat the Rangers five-nothing. It was nothing short of a rout. Outside the main gate of Hampden, broken-hearted Rangers supporters made a bonfire of their flags : it was the dark night of the soul. Year after year, Rangers went down in one stage or other of the competition. It became a national joke. Famous Rangers players, laden with international honours, retired from the team without a single Cup medal.

When success came, it was doubly sweet, for they met and overcame Celtic in the Final. The Princess pantomime had a comic sketch that year of Rangers as Cup winners. Naturally enough, the Christmas pantomime was still running when the Final was played in April, and the comedian came on to the stage, wearing a Rangers jersey, and carrying, not the usual comedy prop, but the Cup itself, the genuine article. There was an enthusiastic uproar. It would be pleasant to think that the ranks of Tuscany could scarce forbear to cheer, but when it comes to cheering the other side, Rangers and Celtic fans can forbear without difficulty.

The monopoly of the Old Firm has been challenged hopefully and repeatedly, but in vain. Airdrie ran into second place in the League and lifted the Cup in the days when great men like Gallacher and McPhail played for them. But the challenge faded, largely because it was too difficult to keep a first-class team together in a devastated area like Airdrie where the home gates were hardly enough to pay the guarantee to the visitors. The same fate downed Motherwell, who did actually win the League on one occasion. No matter how brilliantly the team played, they had to rely on away gates, Cup drawings and the profits from foreign tours to keep the wolf away from the Board-room door. Motherwell's most prosperous year was also their saddest. They met Celtic in the Cup Final and were leading by two clear goals ten minutes from the end. Then Celtic scored one goal and launched an attack which caused indescribable confusion and excitement. At one point the referee ran for shelter behind the goal to escape from the Celtic players, who were tearing the jacket off him in their anxiety to make it quite clear that they considered his ruling unsatis-factory. Almost in the last gasp of the game a harrassed Motherwell defender put the ball through his own goal, and that meant a replay. Everybody knew Motherwell were finished. Celtic never miss a second chance.

Indeed, for all Motherwell's admirable skill, they always lacked the dour persistence of the Old Firm. If the Old Firm are well set for the League or the Cup, they are fairly sure to win. They don't turn dizzy as other teams do ; they have the habit of success.

Of course, consistency in the League has an economic background. It depends on an ample supply of absolutely first-class reserves and only a wealthy club can afford to keep valuable players on a string. Hearts are the wealthiest team in Scotland, and for a generation men turned their eyes towards Tynecastle in the hope of finding a formidable and permanent challenge to the Old Firm monopoly.

Hearts are the deepest mystery in Scottish football. They fail not so much ingloriously as ridiculously. Their faithful supporters cheer frantically while they run rings round Rangers or bundle Celtic home ignominiously, and next Saturday there comes to Edinburgh the dismal news that the heroes have collapsed before the worried onslaught of some humble team struggling in the slums at the bottom of the League Table. It used to be said that Hearts flattered to deceive, but that is no longer true. They flatter in vain ; they deceive no more.

The biggest event of the year is, of course, the match with England. Scotland holds a handsome lead in these games, and we are still nearly certain to beat England any year at Hampden, where the fierce roar which spurs on the home team sounds to the English like a lynching chorus. But our record at Wembley is rather poor. We started with a very brilliant victory and followed it with an equally emphatic defeat, since when we have done no better than draw. The difference between English and Scottish football is very real. It is instinctive. You can see it in boys playing in the street. But we have taught the English more than we have learned from them and our superiority is not what it was.

Indeed the ancients and the prophets maintain that Scottish football is in hopeless decline. The point might be argued happily for ever. But, if football is less precise and elegant than it used to be, it by no means follows that it is less effective. Sometimes one reads that a team has delighted the crowd by a display of perfect, pre-War proof football and been beaten by three or four goals. It is perhaps significant that first-class teams play their most scientific and decorative game when the going is easy.

Whatever may be said about the quality of post-War football, there can be no denying that it is uncommonly poor in " characters." Scotland lost something more rare than a fine player when J. B. McAlpine hung up his large boots and finally quitted the field where he had entertained both friend and foe for many happy years. The average contemporary player is a humdrum person. He wears a bowler hat. He plays golf. Football has become suburbanised. The big games are patronised by the Rugby clientele. Some day, it may be, the fans will bring rugs with them and hot-water bottles, instead of screw-tops. But so long as Celtic and Rangers continue to dispute the passage of the historic Ulster stream, the hot-water bottles will be of the hardware variety which can have a more sudden and startling effect when applied to the head than they ever have on the feet.

by

R. N. BILES

The game is not always more than its players. Here one who has played Rugby with perseverance and writes about it with distinction, recalls some of the personalities who have given the game its flavour

RUGBY FOOTBALL

RUGBY football has never been so popular in Scotland as it is to-day. Its popularity as a spectacle may have been greater a few seasons ago when there were more spectacular sides than we have now, but the game as a game is growing. There are more new clubs, new players, new grounds than ever before. Perhaps the most impressive of all these new things are the new grounds. It is possible—though I should not care to press the theory very far—that these new grounds—many of them belonging to clubs of established tradition—so well drained and laid out, so beautifully turfed and well cared for, have contributed to the destruction of the traditional Scottish forward game of massed dribbling of the ball which flourished on heavy going and was one of the major glories of many a Saturday afternoon's match. We do not see much of this sort of thing now, and we may see even less in the future.

All these new grounds, of course, have their new stands, too, and very commodious some of them are, though scarcely comfortable. The rigours of the game are not all endured by the players. Even Murrayfield's stand, that great whale's belly of steel and concrete, makes no concessions to human frailty. One pays ten shillings to see an international there, and one has no more room for body and legs than can be bought for sixpence in the gallery of a theatre.

Yet the fear of hard seats and cramp in the legs has not kept many comfort-loving persons away from Murrayfield. In recent years international matches have grown in importance as social occasions, and not all the women who go to Murrayfield to see who's there and to enliven the tedium of the afternoon with gossip are so well-informed as that small but critical and knowledgeable band of matrons who are, or were until recently, faithful spectators at one of the Glasgow grounds.

They know the game and they know the players, and they have all the ruthlessness one associates with women ambitious for their own. " Sink him, Mackenzie," they cry, or " Give them more boot, forwards." Yet they lack the spartan outlook of women supporters of the Border clubs, for whom the game is greater than the players. A year or two ago, one of the Border sides was playing in Glasgow, and a Borderer was hurt in a tackle, so badly indeed that he had to be carried off the ground. They bore him away shoulder high as if he had been a dead chieftain, and as the cortège passed along the front of the stand one of three girls who had travelled with the visiting side stood up to get a better view of the victim. She took one glance at the face white with pain and sat down in evident relief. " Ach, it's only Tommy," she said. " He's done onywey."

We are not all so single-minded in our devotion to the game. Rugby spectators are hero-worshippers, and Saturday afternoons are never so bright after the particular Tommy they admire has accepted the verdict that he is " done." Not long ago I saw the great

The Face of Scotland : Winter in a Highland Glen

The Face of Scotland : Summer on Deeside near Braemar

J. M. Bannerman at a match. He never existed for me except as a player. When he retired I almost thought of him as being dead, and it seemed shocking that he should be sitting in the stand and not leading the Glasgow High School forwards in one of their feared and famous rushes.

He is the most celebrated of all Scottish post-War players. There may have been forwards who excelled him in this phase or that of the game, and some maintain that D. S. Davies of Hawick was a better all-rounder. But Davies, splendid forward that he was, played a mere 20 games for Scotland. Bannerman's tally was 37 games. He was little more than a boy when he was first chosen for Scotland in the 1920-1 season, and he never missed a match until he appeared for the last time at Murrayfield against England in 1929. When he retired people felt that something had gone from the game that never could be replaced. Though there was a good deal of sentiment in this reflection, there was also more than a little truth. Bannerman was the embodiment of the traditional Scottish forward game.

H. S. Mackintosh, who played one season with Bannerman, carried on the tradition for three or four years. He, too, looked as if he had been carved from the solid, and like Bannerman he was a born leader. His deep voice baying, " Well done, lads !" would have rallied the dead. Neither he nor Bannerman was conspicuously big or clever. But they were strong and tireless.

Personality is the patina that enriches the bright colours of talent. Bannerman and Mackintosh had it, so had those three grand Border forwards, J. W. Allan, W. B. Welsh and J. Beattie, the last still happily in the game and the most popular player in Scotland. All of them were "characters." To see Welsh at the line-out with his sleeves pulled up, spitting on his hands and clapping them to encourage the forwards in another effort, was to be reminded that Rugby is a democratic game. Yet since forwards perform their prodigies of strength and valour in that whirl of arms and legs which is the scrum, they are rarely such heroes to the crowd as the backs who give the game its flow and rhythm. No four forwards have yet become such legendary figures as I. S. Smith, G. P. S. Macpherson, G. G. Aitken and A. C. Wallace, the Oxford three-quarter line who played for Scotland in the 1923-4-5 seasons. Aitken returned to his native New Zealand, and Wallace to Australia (though he came back as captain of the 1927-8 New South Wales Waratahs), but Macpherson and Smith were for many seasons as famous a partnership at three-quarter as H. Waddell and J. B. Nelson were at half-back.

Smith outstayed Macpherson. He was indeed the last survivor of what now seem to be the golden years of post-War Rugby, and when he played his last game at Murrayfield against England in 1933 the slim young man had become almost burly, and the complete wing three-quarter, not quite so fast as he had been, but still able to score tries in the grand manner. As a younger player he had little to contribute to the game but his great stride (which was not surprising in one who had been brought up to Association football at Winchester) and he had needed all Macpherson's skill to make him a player.

Macpherson could play excruciatingly badly, and he was no man for a wet day or for the vehemence of an Irish match, but he is the greatest personality of the last twenty years. He was strikingly handsome, which international players usually are not, and a graceful and beautifully balanced runner. He had no use for the game as mere violence. His was a first-class brain, and he played Rugby as much as an intellectual exercise as a physical one. It was indeed as if he were playing a sort of running-about chess, for he could think two moves ahead of his opponents and often of his own side as well. On his day the perfect co-ordination of hand and brain and eye made the rough-and-tumble of the game seem sport for ploughmen.

J. C. Dykes was another of Macpherson's celebrated contemporaries, and like him a player of erratic performance. He was born gay, and while he patently enjoyed success he was unperturbed by failure. He could do the brilliant thing, or in one of his moods of happy irresponsibility the foolish one, but the game was always a game to him, never an international crisis. His fellow Glasgow Academicals, Waddell and Nelson, took the business more seriously. Nelson when the game was halted often seemed the embodiment of dejection, standing with his shoulders drooping, arms hanging at his sides, looking a little like that well-known picture of the poor horse tied up in the snow outside the inn while his master is boozing inside. But once the game was on again, Nelson came to life, throwing out his cannon-ball passes to Waddell, or sneaking away on the blind side of the scrum like a furtive guest from a tedious party, with a hammer-blow of a hand-off for the forward who tried to hold him up.

Scotland has been fortunate in scrum half-backs. There was Nelson to succeed W. E. Bryce and W. R. Logan to follow him, but the partnership of Waddell and Nelson has yet to be equalled. Waddell may not have been quite so quick off his mark as the tough and resilient H. Lind, but he was a far better team player, and a more successful bedeviller of defences. His opponents must often have shaken their heads at the recollection of the number of different ways in which he had fooled them, and his dropped goals are still spoken of with respect.

This sketch must end, with much left unsaid, and many great players uncelebrated—D. Drysdale, for example, whose talent for the full-back position amounted to genius. Rugby football uses up its players at a faster rate than most sports, and the annals of the game are rich in names and personalities. Nothing has been said of the famous club sides of the last twenty years—Watsonians, Edinburgh Academicals, Heriot's, Glasgow Academicals, Glasgow High School, and Hawick, clubs who by tradition are expected to dominate the game ; and those two others, Dunfermline and Hillhead High School, who in their vintage years astonished and delighted their friends by their meteoric brilliance.

And nothing has been said, either, of that vast anonymous band of players who make up the second and third, the fourth and fifth fifteens of the clubs. Not for them the distinction of newspaper headlines ; their names are never seen in print. They play on grounds which, if some of them are better than they used to be, are often waterlogged and ankle deep in mud. There are no spectators to encourage them, they are lucky if their games are graced by two touch judges ; the referee is sometimes chosen more for his good-natured willingness to lend a hand than for his knowledge or judgment. But enthusiasm sustains them in all these trials, and it is they who are and will remain the backbone of the game.

by
S. L. McKINLAY

A well-known International Golfer discusses the recent developments of the game, and particularly the way in which young players dominate International and Championship meetings

GOLF : THE YOUNG MAN'S GAME

IT is one of the paradoxes of what we choose to call modern civilisation that golf, which is, with the possible exception of croquet and chess, the most leisurely of pastimes, should not only have retained its popularity in this age of speed but should even have increased it.

The game has not, of course, escaped unscathed. It is no longer the prerogative of the middle-aged and old, to be played in measured elegance at a pace in keeping with the age of the players. Rather has it become more intense, more an affair of energy, mental and physical, than it was a generation ago. It still, such is the nature of the game, requires at least a two hours' traffic of the links ; for those zealots who play a dozen rounds in a day, clad in a pair of shorts and running shoes and carrying only one club, are hardly of the true race of golfers.

But the so-called friendly game, which our fathers played so debonairly, has become tainted with the modern lust for efficiency. There are more competitions, tournaments, and championships to provide tests for that efficiency, and no one is too old or too young to enter the arena. The Boys' and Girls' Championships cater for the babes and sucklings of the links ; the Seniors have their own championships ; and no club, however humble, is so far behind the times as not to include a veterans' class each monthly medal day. The rigour of the game has extended with its growth in popularity, and Scotland, the spiritual home of golf (whatever the historians may say about the actual origins) has shared in these movements.

There were signs of such developments in the pre-War years, so I am told, but it is only in comparatively recent times that golf has attained a full flowering, for better or worse. For this progress one factor more than any other is responsible—the alteration (I do not say improvement) in the equipment of the players. Technically, I suppose, improvement is the correct word, for no one will deny that modern golf clubs and golf balls are, as instruments, infinitely superior to those our fathers employed.

The modern golf clubs, with their shining steel and coloured twiddly bits, and the modern golf ball, which flatters the most scuffling stroke, have made of golf a much less difficult affair than it used to be. Even the least athletic of humans can make a brave show of skill and strength when equipped with matched sets of clubs that are so cunningly constructed that they do everything but play the shot as it were *in vacuo*. And the modern " rabbit " ball will scuttle along a trim fairway half as far again as the early rubber-cored ball and twice as far as the unresponsive, uncompromising gutta ball.

Perhaps the clubs have had more to do with golf's popularity than even the ball. The elixir of steel, which was removed from the poison list in November 1929, brought new golfing life to millions. At an age when it was deemed inevitable that bowls, not golf, should be a man's game he found that the steel shaft had not only arrested the march of time but had even restored the years which seemed to have gone for ever. Whereas he used to play only nine holes, and these not very well, now he can play a full round of eighteen with all the vigour he possessed in his hey-day.

Yet, although golf is more of an old man's game than ever before, in the past ten years or so the ball has been at the feet of the young men. Particularly is this true of Scotland, where the tournament winner over thirty is regarded as an anachronism. Only the professionals, strangely enough, have resisted the challenge of youth ; yet even this stronghold has in recent years been invaded and the winners of the Scottish Professional Championship in 1936 and 1937 were in their twenties. Even the ladies, of whom it is considered doubtful etiquette to inquire the age, have given youth a blank cheque, and in the last ten years only three of the winners might have had a reasonable excuse for declining to disclose how long they had been playing this most fascinating and most exasperating game.

But it is among the amateurs that Scottish golf has blossomed most abundantly in the last decade, and all, I think, because of the reprehensible practice of labelling players of distinction. Let me explain. In the old days it was deemed bad form to inquire too closely into a man's social standing. If he were an Army man, like the great F. G. Tait, there was, of course, no harm in describing him as " the gallant soldier," even if his play were most ungallant (although this did not apply to Tait). Now, however, it is not sufficient that a man should be a good golfer. He must be known as " the prosperous meat salesman from Glasgow," " the blond young whisky salesman," " the dark-haired University student," " the horny-handed son of toil straight from the coal face," and so on.

This is, of course, an American importation, and as such is to be deplored, but the practice has, as I have suggested, had a salutary effect on Scottish amateur golf. On a certain day in the early summer of 1926 a young Glasgow golfer named Andrew Jamieson had the audacity to defeat one R. T. Jones, of U.S.A., in the Amateur Championship at Muirfield. Now Jamieson was, and still is, a very good golfer indeed, but Jones was, and probably still is, a better. The American's eclipse was a golfing " bombshell," and the repercussions have not yet spent themselves. Jamieson was known from that day as " the man who beat Bobby Jones," and the label has had much more effect on his contemporaries than on the man who made it possible.

It made the young men of Scottish golf see visions of triumph and dream dreams of championship victories. The stimulus was timely. Scotland had not won the Amateur Championship since the year that War broke out, for Robert Harris, who won in 1925, was an Anglo-Scot of many years' adoption. Scotland had not even been faring well in the annual international matches with England. Scottish golf was, in short, at a low ebb, and the tide looked as if it might recede further. From 1926 onwards, however, the tide has turned, and in recent years it has been taken at the flood and has brought fame, if not fortune, to several young Scottish golfers.

It has produced perhaps the best amateur golfer who never won the Amateur Championship and who cannot now win it—Jack McLean. In the same year as Jamieson beat Jones, McLean won his first tournament of any consequence, the now defunct West of

Scotland Boys' Championship. In the next ten years he was to win the Scottish Amateur Championship three times in successive years, and reach the final in the fourth year; he twice won the Irish Open Amateur Championship; he won the Australian Amateur Championship, and, in 1936, did what only two British golfers had done in a quarter of a century, reached the final of the American Amateur Championship. And all before he was twenty-six years old.

Even before McLean shot across the golfing firmament, however, Scotland had reasserted itself in the international arena. In 1929 the international match with England was halved, and a week later a Scot, J. N. Smith, reached the final of the Amateur Championship. Two years later, in 1931, Scotland beat England for the first time for many years, and that victory has been repeated every year since, until England must regard the international match with some of the feelings with which Oxford took the tideway for so many years until last year.

Still, Scotland had not won the most prized of all golfing honours, the Amateur Championship. In 1936, however, a slim young Scotsman (as Hector Thomson was invariably described) became Amateur Champion at St Andrews, and the first Scot to win the title on a Scottish links since R. Maxwell beat C. K. Hutchison at Muirfield in 1909. The wheel had turned full circle, a very full circle indeed, for Thomson was the first former Boys' Champion ever to win the Amateur Championship. Youth had been served, and all, I think, because another slim young Scotsman had become "the man who beat Bobby Jones."

But the amateur players have not made a corner in the glories of the game. The ladies have played their part. They do not now approach their international matches with an overwhelming sense of inferiority ; they think nothing of beating the three other countries, although they hardly do it with the same facility or intensity of purpose as the men. In their championship, too, they are bidding fair to redress the balance of power. For long, particularly in the brave days of Miss Leitch and Miss Wethered as was, the best they could hope for was a bronze medal. And then, in 1934, Mrs A. M. Holm, a Scottish Champion of 1930 and 1932, won the British Championship on a Welsh course from an English opponent. Better was to follow last year, however, for not only did a slim Scots girl (to maintain the sequence) win the Championship on a Scots course, but from a Scots opponent, another slim Scots girl. Miss Anderson, last year's champion, may be described as the Jack McLean of women's golf, for although she has not reached the final of the U.S. Women's Championship she has won the New Zealand Championship and the French Open Championship.

The moral seems to be, not—join the Army and see the world, but play golf and see the world.

SOME CHARACTERS

by
JAMES FERGUSSON

In a collection of Scottish characters
we must include the Eighteenth
Century Laird, whose holy enthusiasm
in draining fields, building roads and
planting trees did so much to civilise
the face of Scotland

PORTRAIT OF A GENTLEMAN

I HAVE known him, in a sense, ever since my childhood. Whenever any of my brothers or I came
home after long absence at school or elsewhere,
it used to be a regular ritual for someone to say, " Have
you said ' How do you do ? ' to Sir Adam yet ? "
Being thus reminded of a neglected duty, one would
go into the dining-room, place oneself opposite to the
big portrait over the black marble Victorian mantel-
piece, and make the established inquiry, accompanied
by a respectful bow. Sometimes this salutation was
extended to his father and grandfather or a few
other favourites among The Ancestors ; but it was to
Sir Adam that one felt chiefly bound to report oneself,
as it were, on revisiting the family roof-tree.

Sir Adam never unbent so far as to return my bow,
though I always glanced up at him to see if he would.
Sometimes—if, for instance, I had been near the bottom
of my class last term—his eye was a trifle cold, sometimes it rested on me with grave approval, occasionally it
looked almost benevolent. But anything approaching to
geniality would have been foreign to the dignified pose
in which Raeburn's brush had set him there, calm and
upright in his big armchair. There he sat—and there,
for that matter, he still sits—in his sober brown coat,
with his hair neatly powdered, his legs, in their black

silk breeches, composedly crossed, his hands, their fingers interlocked, resting on his knee, and his chair turned a little aside from the table on which lies the letter he has just been reading. He looks exactly the figure described in his obituary notice of October 1813 —" this venerable and respectable Baronet."

It was many years before I came—I might almost say " presumed "—to make Sir Adam's closer acquaintance. The outlines of his life, the fact that he died a bachelor at the age of 80, and a few family traditions illustrating the extreme propriety of his conduct— these at least were familiar to me ; and I was dimly aware that he had been a great planter of trees and had laid out most of our favourite paths through the surrounding woods. The phrase " in Sir Adam's time," applied to plantations, paths, or farmhouses, denoted to me a vague epoch a little subsequent to the Creation ; and it was beyond my youthful imagination to conceive what appearance the hills and woods of my home might have borne before his constructive hand had been laid upon them. He remained a kind of peak in history, an eminent and dominating figure of the past. No doubt Raeburn's art, and the position of his portrait in the place of honour, had much to do with forming this impression.

I knew that in certain long drawers in another room there lay a vast collection of Sir Adam's correspondence ; but it was not until a few years ago that I began to explore them. What I found there introduced me for the first time to the vivid realities of life in eighteenth century Scotland. It taught me that history was not after all a dead thing belonging only to the past. And also it led me at last to appreciate the significance of that letter on the table in Sir Adam's portrait.

Sir Adam had been what is known as a voluminous correspondent. From about 1756 till a few months before his death he seemed to have preserved almost every letter of importance he received, and, in many cases, copies of his answers. From this mass of documents and some research in books, it was possible to piece together in fascinating detail large periods of his industrious life in the Scotland of Boswell and Burns : his " grand tour " as a young man, his interests and friendships, his career at the Scottish Bar and in Parliament, and his loving and methodical care for the family estate to which he succeeded in 1759.

For several years now the exploration and reconstruction of Sir Adam's life has been one of my major interests. I have not yet got to the end of his correspondence. Sometimes I doubt if I ever shall. He was a man who never left a letter unanswered, and seldom wrote in one sentence what could be more politely expressed in three. Many people would call him a dull correspondent. To me he is a perpetual delight. As he winds his way through clause within clause of each elaborate paragraph, with that neat and flourishing handwriting, as careful in his old age as in his youth, and with grammar so faultless and punctuation so meticulous that any one of his letters might be printed without editing as it stands, I follow him with the appreciation of a musical critic listening to the unravelling of a well scored fugue. To-day I know him as intimately as a favourite uncle ; and neither long-windedness, formality, nor an almost total absence of humour obscures my admiration of him.

His letters contain no original thoughts, and his frequent good advice to his nephew and heir consists chiefly of gracefully expressed platitude. But his sincerity is never in doubt ; his advice, if trite, is invariably sound, for he was a very wise and sensible man ; and no one practised more thoroughly the virtues of honesty, industry and public service which he preached. He deserved Burns's eulogy of him— " aith-detesting, chaste Kilkerran "—and he was too sympathetic to be a prig.

I will not write of his long political career—he was a good politician but not made for a statesman—nor of the entertaining but complicated electioneering intrigues which form the subject of many of his letters. Nor, for the sake of space, will I touch on his clashes with Boswell, his friendship with that versatile and charming man George Dempster of Dunnichen (whose letters to him I have published elsewhere) or their tireless efforts, including an arduous journey through the greater part of the Hebrides, to work out a scheme for checking Highland emigration by establishing fishing-stations on the West Coast. Sir Adam's long life and wide acquaintance with politicians and men of letters would fill a book. It is only one side of his busy career that concerns me now : the activities that transformed the fields, woods, and roads of his corner of Ayrshire, and thereby provided his most enduring memorial.

Sir Adam was one of the " improving " lairds—a body of men which has never, I think, received proper recognition for the services they rendered to Scotland, though a great deal of what is good in rural Scotland to-day is due to their labours. " Improving " often ran in families, and it did so in Sir Adam's. His father—a Lord of Session—was planting trees, turning moorland into pasture, and laying out policies away back in George I.'s time. His younger brother, also

CHARACTER

a judge, the amiably impulsive Lord Hermand, became rather late in life an improver in his turn, and farmed in West Lothian with a zeal which was almost fanatical. Sir Adam's own improvements were business-like and thorough. A full account of the earlier ones is given in Andrew Wight's *Recent State of Husbandry in Scotland*, whose author, when he visited Carrick in 1777, " saw various operations of husbandry carried on with industry and attention, the inclosures in perfection, both hedges and stone walls," and praised the " progress of agriculture in that part of the country " as being " chiefly owing to Sir Adam himself."

Sir Adam, in a letter to Wight, recalled the backward state of agriculture in Carrick a few years earlier, " when there was scarce an inclosure in it but some few round the gentlemen's houses, when there was not a pound of grass seed sown from one end of it to the other, and when the whole attention of the farmer, and the whole dung of the farm, was applied to a few acres, while the rest was totally neglected."

I can give no better account of Sir Adam's improvements than his own, which is more directly and economically expressed than many of his private letters :

" My object has been to turn the farms in my own possession into good grass as soon as possible. . . . The trouble and expense that I have bestowed on this object has been much greater than any person would conceive from the quantity of ground that I have improved, without considering what it was in its natural state. You cannot fail to have observed the multitude of large stones upon the uncultivated fields in this country ; most of these are of such a size as to require being blasted with gun-powder before they are carried off. As the soil runs naturally to wood, there is a necessity of clearing the fields of shrubs and bushes before they can be properly ploughed. If to this is added the expense of draining, you will not be surprised at my saying that many fields cost more than their original price before the plough is put into the ground."

By the 1780's, however, all the farms on the estate were enclosed, and the wasteful old run-rig system was a thing of the past. Pasture had greatly improved, and the farmers had learnt, by example, the importance of keeping their land in good heart. Lime was made available in large quantities from a quarry on the estate. The breed of sheep also had been much improved by the importation of Dorchester and Bakewell rams. Elaborate draining had been carried out on the lower ground, and hundreds of acres had been planted with trees.

At the end of the century Sir Adam's correspondence shows him busy with road-making, linking up his neighbourhood with Maybole and Ayr to the north and Girvan to the south, and providing an outlet for the coal which Hamilton of Bargany, Kennedy of Dunure, and the Earl of Cassillis were working on their respective properties on the north side of the valley. He built two high stone bridges over the Water of Girvan, of simple and beautiful design, which still stand to-day as good as new. In these days, when Government and local authorities make roads with public money, it is often forgotten how much, a hundred and fifty years ago, was left, and sometimes very successfully left, to private enterprise. When I watch the buses speeding northwards beside the Water of Girvan, I often recall with a secret pleasure that their unconscious passengers are travelling not only beneath Sir Adam's trees and beside his fields, but over one of his bridges and along his road, made by his initiative, according to his plan, and largely at his expense.

To these activities Sir Adam devoted his declining and gout-ridden years, combining with them the care of a large family of nephews and nieces of two generations who looked up to him as to a father. He owned himself " heartily tired " of Parliament, and declined the offer of Henry Dundas (suggested by George III. himself) that he should go to India as Governor of Madras. With an occasional grumble of a kind grown more common since his day—" this Income Tax is a galling one "—he settled down to spend the rest of his life at home. " *Ille terrarum*," he might have quoted, " *mihi praeter omnes angulus ridet* " ; and he found everything about it perfect, even the climate. " There is not probably a milder air in the winter months than that in which I now sit," he wrote in January 1809 ; and in another letter, written in a similar season, he sums up the contentment of his quiet but still active life :

" We have had a delightful winter . . . without snow, of which we have not had three days during the whole season. The air is now delightful, and the birds singing as in spring. Five or six large trees were blown down here ; among which one of the largest beeches above the house. But enough remain : and I think, upon a moderate computation, for every one blown down, I plant 5000."

by
GEORGE BURNETT

The Scottish nation has always been
rich in Eccentrics, who may have been
a little mad, but were wise enough
to get their own way through being
different from other people. Such as
Dainty Daniel

DAINTY DANIEL

NOBODY knew the story of Dainty's life beyond the time he came to the Howe o' Buchan. A bitter day of smoor drift it was, as my mother used to tell, with the milk standing frozen a quarter of an inch thick in the afternoon. She was thawing out a little for a cup of tea when a rattle came to the door. She gave no heed to the noise, supposing it was the storm trying to come in. Then there was a scratching on the window and she could see two beads of eyes looking in on her through the lacework of frost. A wanchancy thing it was. First she thought of the cat, but there was Bluekins straiked out like a dead hare in front of the glowing peats. Next she barred the door for fear it was some weird wanting to mischief her.

On the back of five she drew the bar, as her man might be home early, and sat down with her face away from the window. A minute or two after the door opened and something clanked over the flag-stones. "For mercy's sake, woman, let me in, or I'll be perished," it whistled, followed by a snell scurry of wind and snow. When she saw what it was she did not know whether to bide in the house or run screaming into the storm. For Dainty looked like nothing in nature. His long beard was fingered with icicles

212

which glinted in the lamp-light; his legs bound in straw rapes up to the knees, and the rest of him swathed in strips of sacking.

"Well, man?" she asked, gripping the back of the chair, and giving a bit hysterical laugh. Then in a more conciliatory tone: "Folk are best inside the nicht."

So she motioned him to a seat, which he sat down on stiffly, as if there were no joints in his body. By-and-by the heat of the fire loosened the scales of ice on him, which pinged clear on the stone below. They melted, forming a rivulet, which zig-zagged across the floor. She waited for him to speak again, but he just sat staring at the kettle crook. It would be half an hour after he came in that he made any motion at all. He began twitching his body as a man does with a mustard-plaster on his back, the movement becoming more and more agitated. Then he stood up and shook himself like a wet dog, and began to unwind the rapes on his legs and last the strips of sacking. These he put in a tidy heap, which steamed up the chimley.

"And noo I could be doin' wi' a cuppie o' tea," he said, smacking his lips expectantly. "Do you hear? I could be doin' wi' something!"

But she let him speak on, knowing him to be nothing better than an impudent gangrel. He drew himself up to the table, smart enough, when she had set her man's supper, but he just had to contain himself with patience until he came home. Dainty did not mix eating and talking. He drew his breath noisily when his cup was empty, and pushed it away from him.

"A little more of your water, guid-wife! I'm very bad at eating anything dry."

That was a fine thing to say about the best tea that

could be bought for money, let alone the insult to a newly opened jar of rhubarb. Dainty ate and drank till my mother got feared for him, so she began clearing the table.

"Steady, lass," he remonstrated. "I'll tell you when I'm finished."

It might have been supposed that he would say something about himself after all that good eating, but he was close as an oyster. Long after people said that he had run away from a crime, but that was unlikely as there was little wickedness in him, except the stealing of a hen now and then. Dainty was just a " puir craytur " whom you could not help pitying. That first night he gave the measure of himself when he said : " If I were a king, I would be a costly king. I'd eat ream brose and ream to them and sleep up to the een amang strae." Fortunate it was that he confided his ambition for it solved the problem of his bedding. It would have been a heartless thing to turn him out until the thaw came.

Without a word of thanks he stalked away like an animated mummy. The next thing they heard about him was that he had taken up house in a gigantic meal girnel on the hillside. Meal girnel it was called, but how anybody could have filled it with meal was a matter for speculation, as indeed it was how a girnel came to be on the hill at all. Dainty's occupation of it soon became an old story. It was the development outside that made people talk. He pulled up the heather and sowed clover, and made bee skeps in such numbers that it was fun counting them. By the time the clover was red he had gotten a raith of bees. Then it came out that Dainty believed that Providence might carry him off to Palestine at any moment. Palestine was a land flowing with milk and honey, and must be a grand place for bees.

From that time Dainty was a man worth watching, especially on a Saturday afternoon. At the time of her spring cleaning Jock Peter's wife had given him her man's swallow-tailed coat and lum hat. They were green with age, it was true, but Dainty was not particular. Every Saturday afternoon he could be seen striding down to the Broch with his head in the air, nose a little in front, as if he were sniffing the sanctity of the morrow. What sect he belonged to nobody knew. Perhaps the Palestine Brethren. It was a twenty-mile walk to the Broch. So Dainty broke his journey at a friendly farmer's steading, covering the remaining five miles in fine style. With both hands plunged in his coat-tails he sang "Jerusalem the Golden, with milk and honey blessed," most of the way, except when he chanced to see a piece of coal on the road. Then he stopped to wrap it up in a bit of newspaper (invariably he carried a newspaper for this purpose) and put it in one of his pockets. By the time he reached the Broch he bulged at the back like a woman in a bustle. He returned to his girnel on the late afternoon of Monday, and might be seen making the round of his skeps before taking off his hat.

A loud guffaw circled the parish when he took to proselytising. But barns were placed at his disposal everywhere. The audience sweated with inward laughter, and Dainty thought their discomfort was due to a conviction of sin. Naturally, he expatiated most on the glories of the Holy Land. One morning they would see the heavens red as clover and hear a great humming. The Almighty would catch up the Faithful, skeps and all, in a cloud. Like a swarm they would fly round till they scented the Queen. Then they would be off like a dart of sunlight to a Land Flowing with Milk and Honey. His eyes gleamed with anticipation : " Only if you're ready, like me ! " A sigh rose among his hearers, and he pleaded with them not to neglect their opportunities. For their encouragement and enlightenment he discoursed on bee culture, showing a knowledge that exceeded that in most text-books. " Consider the bee and be wise ! " he paraphrased ; " and don't forget the price of honey."

But Dainty was not a one-text man. He loved to describe the psychological processes of Daniel in the Den of Lions. He painted with harrowing detail the uneasy sleep of the king who had cast Daniel into the Den. Neither were instruments of music brought to him, not even the trump ! He got up early in the morning fair beside himsel' wondering whether there would be anything left of Daniel in addition to his watch-chain. To his terror and amazement there was Daniel gripping the throats o' a king o' beasts to right and left o' him, wi' a bit kick now and then at the more inquisitive o' the others. " Aye, Daniel was a boy to be proud of. Exactly like me. Not that I've ever been put to it—there's nae lions within a hundred miles o' here—but I ken fine how to settle their snash. If anyone would like to growl at me I'll demonstrate. Even with the closing and opening of the hands."

Dainty surveyed the audience hopefully, plucking the air in a sort of five-finger exercise. The compressed lips and puffed cheeks which he saw were signs to him of cowardice and not of internal combustion. The majority of his hearers could have laid Dainty over their knees and snapped him like a dry stick. The two minutes or so that he gloated over them were almost unendurable, and several bowed their heads to hide their faces.

" You may well repent, Alex Davidson, and you, Will Means, and you——," cried Dainty, naming those who were most affected. " You're all feared o' Daniel and ken fu' brawly that you're miserable sinners . . ."

" There's a strong connection between lions and bees. You mind Samson ? He was steppin' doon to Timnath one day when a great big lion roared at him. What did he dae but tear the gomeril in twa halves as you micht a bit paper. The next time he was in that part o' the world he turned aside to see the carcase, and lo and behold ! it was a bees' bike."

Dainty had his set days for visiting. So certain was he in his movements that he might have served as calendar and clock. He carried an oat sack on his back for the reception of the tea, sugar, oatmeal, and other things that he begged. Each pickle he wrapped up in newspaper, screwing the top of the package into a spiral. Unlike other going-about men, he was not grateful for small mercies. Immediately he came in he announced what he " could be doing with." If told that there was a shortage of the wanted commodity he hummed and hawed and was most uncivil. It was for this reason that he got the nickname of Dainty and sometimes Pike-thank, and many people got very tired of him. When he noticed this he began bringing the children little pretty things he had made himself. The most cherished of these were harps fashioned from the pith of rushes and bird-cages of the same material. There were two types of the latter, one plain and the other ornamented, with an artificial bee swinging on a trapeze.

As he expected and got a meal of some kind at each

house he visited, the wonder grew what became of the proceeds of his begging. There was also the mystery of how he disposed of his honey—now considerable in amount. It was said that he had it carted away in the early hours of the morning, but no one had seen this happen or even noticed a cart track.

Dainty stopped going his rounds in August 1885. So sudden a break in habit was commented on from end to end of the parish and necks were stretched on the next Saturday afternoon for the familiar swallow-tail and lum-hat bobbing down to the Broch. Something was wrong. Either Daniel had disappeared as mysteriously as he had come or he was ill—perhaps dead. As no one had dared to call on him during his residence in the girnel, even out of curiosity, there was much discussion as to how he should be approached. A young man volunteered to leave a pail of beef-tea outside. It was there next day, unopened. Then he took three eggs, and the shells were found a little distance away, sucked clean by weasels.

At last six or seven determined to break down the door. They approached the girnel in open formation as they would have done a strong post in war. They need not have bothered, for Dainty was dead, and would not have harmed them had he been alive. There he lay on his bed of heather and straw as straight as an ice tangle. Outside the hill was a blaze of purple, the air vibrated with the drone of heavily laden bees. They took Dainty and buried him where his heart had been ; and next evening the men's wives crawled one at a time into the girnel to see what it was like inside. Round the walls ran a number of shelves on which stood countless little newspaper packets carefully screwed at the top. For decoration there were two greasy oleographs of Jerusalem and Daniel in the Den of Lions, and a large chart showing the structure of the bee. In a corner lay a pile of rapes and strips of sacking which one of the curious turned over with a stick. Beneath it lay a wooden box containing ninety golden sovereigns and just over twenty pounds in silver !

by
J. S. BUIST

The Scots have also been a people of imagination. But that has been shown more in the written than the spoken word. As in this case of David

IMAGINATION

HOW he slipped into my memory again this week I cannot explain. Certainly it was no recollection of his outward appearance that brought him back to me. It must be ten years at least since I as much as thought of him, and as many more before that since I last saw him. What he was like I cannot recollect, perhaps because a child, readily receptive to the half-monumental figures of the grown-up people of its world, takes little heed of the faces of other children. Probably his name was David, probably he was about two years older than myself—eight or nine to my six or seven. Everything about his appearance has faded now—his build, his colouring, his voice. All that remains distinct is the impression of his strong imagination, which, now that I come to think of it, makes him, boy though he was and boy though he will always remain for me, the most perfect liar I have ever met.

If David himself is vague in recollection, his setting, so much that of my own childhood, remains clear. The village on the southern bank of the river estuary had not yet begun its evolution into a suburb. No one had yet thought of sweeping away David's home as an obstruction to traffic. Its steep stair—the house was above a cellar that had been a stable in the change-house days—jutted out into the road and made a bottleneck, as a toll-house should, right in the middle of the village. If the carts and gigs were sometimes held up there, nobody very much cared ; it was as good a place as any to pass the time of day. Across the road the three-acre field was still a market garden, and there David's father worked. He was a tall man, bowed a little at the shoulders from a lifetime of planting and digging. He seldom spoke, and he dominated the garden with his silence just as his wife dominated the house and the narrow of the road with her shrill complaining.

These two and their milieu, garden and house, are as plain to me as yesterday ; as pungent in the memory as the smell of the leaves David's father burned in October. Bob, their elder son, apprenticed to a saddler, is less distinct, remembered more for an aroma of corduroy and dubbin and a passion for fireworks than for any physical properties. David, the younger son, is least clear of all, with only the strength of his imagination to save him from oblivion.

David was more than a mere liar ; his imagination had its practical side that found expression in action. Now that the three-acre field is a playing-ground the boys of the village probably play football in the summer evenings, perhaps even cricket ; but David and those of us who played with him knew nothing of either football or cricket. We had other ploys, most of them, it must be admitted, of David's devising.

It was David who first discovered that a tin can battered on to the end of a stick looks like the leg of a horse, and he was first when ten or a dozen of us so equipped made cavalry charges along the farm road. It was David who saw in a rock on the beach the likeness of a ship, and it was he who had us all on board, evening after evening for weeks, manning the "Titanic" under his command. It was David who started us digging down to Australia. It was David who had us damming the field ditches for gold. The commonplace of children's play, all these ; yet to be real they had to be spontaneous. In David's quick mind we found our spontaneity. Every new discovery was his.

Yet these are the details that came last to my mind when I tried to piece together all I could recall about David. It was his lies, the artistic rather than the practical expression of his imagination, that I remembered first. And it was artistic. David did not lie because he gained anything by it, nor, so far as I can remember, as a means of escape from punishment. He lied as an artist — for lying's sake and for the impression he knew he could produce.

That the greater lies may be the more credible I will narrate the smaller first. Such was the "robber's den," the cottage at the foot of our garden, where Mrs Duke lived, who called us in on baking-days and gave us handfuls of crumbly new bannock. In Mrs Duke's house had lived a band of robbers, with Mrs Duke's grandfather for their leader, and had harried the roads by day and the river by night. David lied with circumstance. This path from the house to the river was theirs. That tile in the roof was smashed when the soldiers, a whole battalion of them, besieged the house. On the oak tree in the garden, the one with the nails in it, the leader was hanged. How long ago ? A long time ago, maybe twenty years. " But mind, don't tell ! " I didn't, and for one or two baking-days I avoided Mrs Duke's.

Some of David's lying can be explained. Part of

it had its inspiration and model in the green pages of the *Boys' Friend*, from which David read me week by week the instalments of the story of the imminent world war. But the story was no more than a model; it was never a mere text-book. When David spoke of war it was not as of something distant. The serial writer's war was at sea and in colonies half the world away; David's was in our river, in our countryside. In the chill of the summer evening he looked up from the story he was reading.

"Look," he cried, pointing to the sand-boat in mid-stream. "You see that boat? A German gun-boat. It's waiting till it's dark. Then it will slip up with the tide, up to the bridge, and in the morning when the London train crosses there will be a great hole right in the middle."

His lying was effective.

"What are you shivering for?" he demanded.

"Just cold," I said.

"All right. We'll go home. But mind, don't tell!"

Next day, when there was no gap in the two-mile span of the bridge and the gunboat was gone, he had an answer to my question.

"They couldn't do it this time. Just spied things out this time. They'll be back yet. But mind . . ."

For weeks I scanned the river every evening from the braes. But I did not tell.

There still remains David's most magnificent lie, a piece of independent invention. It was produced to meet and overwhelm my own perfectly true description of a model steamer my uncle had built, which had real engines and went under her own steam. It was nothing to David's steamer.

" Only that big ! " he cried. " Mine's twice that. Yes ! Engines and life-boats, too, and saloons and smoke-rooms." (The local ferryboat was the limit of our joint ideas on nautical matters). " And has your uncle's boat got a crew of little men that wind up and do everything a real man can do ? "

I admitted defeat. David elaborated. The little men were just like human beings.

" Yesterday one of them wouldn't work, and when I told him to get out of the saloon he just swore, and let fly at me with the book he was reading—they have little books of their own, didn't I tell you ?—and hit me on the hand. Here's the scratch."

There the scratch was. When could I see this boat ? David shook his head.

" I'd show it to you if I could, but you see, it's locked away in the wardrobe drawer with my father's good suit, and it's only out on Sundays. I don't get to play with it other days."

That was an end of it. On Sundays we never played together. It was out of the question that I should ever see the ship.

So David lied. Did I believe him ? At this distance in time it seems likely that I did not so much believe him as refrain from disbelieving him ; I think I guessed that his stories were not true, and yet kept on hoping that they were. But that does not alter one whit the validity of that gift of David's. I have said he lied with circumstance. Like Defoe, he " lied like truth." What was far away he brought near, what was vague he made solid, what was unconvincing became certainty on his lips. His potentialities as an imaginative writer, one would say, were beyond doubt.

I have not seen David for more than twenty years. I

have forgotten his surname, and the Christian name I have tacked on to him may not be his. The village is a suburb now. Neither of us lives there. What has become of David? Once, indirectly and uncertainly, I heard that he had done well at school and had gone into a bank, improving on his gardener father and his saddler brother. But what I did not hear was that his imagination, the most remarkable I have ever come across, had ever been the slightest use to him.

by
R. N. BILES

You can hardly imagine a book about
Scottish life that did not mention (*a*)
old buses, and (*b*) Saturday night.
Here these characteristics of our state
are combined in a nice piece of
entertainment

SWEET SATURDAY NIGHT

Sweet Saturday night,
When the week's work is done.—Old Song.

YOU cannot afford to be fastidious in your choice
of transport when you are twelve miles or more
from Glasgow and it is late on a Saturday
night. So long as the vehicle you board appears to
be capable of sustained motion you must step as hopefully into a tumbril as an Elijah's chariot.

Yet having made your bed, you may at least look
around you with disdain or dismay before you lie on
it. And as I groped my way to a seat in the 'bus that
had come rattling over the cobbles I was filled with
misgivings about the pleasures of travel during the next
forty minutes. The 'bus was a museum piece, so old
that it should have been preceded by a man carrying
a flag. It was a tumbril indeed. And from what I
could make out of my travelling companions they were
as fine a set of malefactors as ever rode to the gibbet.
But that was a first impression. The mingling odours
of cigarette smoke, fish and chips, and warm bodies dull
one's perceptions of the essential nobility of man. In
such an atmosphere a squadron of archangels might
well convey an impression of unbounded rascality.
There were no wings or shining armour among my
fellow-passengers.

226

Nor was that all. The deplorable conclusions inspired by the foul air were heightened by the presence of a man playing an accordion to which most of the company were singing with spirit. The normal decorum of the Scot and his traditional liking for whisky often lead one to attribute public displays of hilarity to the bottle. So that I feared for the moment that I was in the presence not merely of rascals but of drunken rascals. The inference proved to be unjust, for although there might have been a dram or two spread thin among the company, they were sober, and with one exception, admirable men indulging, as is fitting on a Saturday night, a natural merriment.

The exception was a negroid young man who sat in a front seat near the accordion player, by this time identified as Charlie. It appeared to be a matter of principle with Charlie that he should play any piece that was called for, but his personal preferences were clearly for familiar Scottish airs and particularly for strathspeys in which he revealed a remarkable virtuosity. I am no connoisseur of the accordion. It is not everybody's instrument, yet it appears to me that its music is heard to perfection in a 'bus. They say of cheese that it digests everything but itself. So with the 'bus. Its noise and rattle mellow all noises but its own. The accordion tends to gustiness, yet this defect and others inherent either in the instrument or the performer are flattened out by the grinding of gears and the rumbling of protesting machinery, so that the resulting music is not only tolerable but pleasant.

But the negroid young man had a voice that was proof against all mellowing, he sang so high and he sang so shrill. His was the authentic voice of Saturday night, the ear-splitting falsetto that fastens on sentimental waltz tunes and overrides the air in a fury of misshapen harmony. It is heard in all the quarters where the common people crowd to take their pleasures. It may rise no higher than a husky croon, or it may have the power and penetration of a ship's siren. It is fed on fish suppers, hot peas and vinegar in Italian ice-cream shops, and cheap seats at the cinema, and its mournful or strident howling expresses a world of unrealised sentiment.

The negroid young man howled as if his heart would break. The song, of his own choosing, was " When you played the organ and I sang 'The Rosary.'" He sprawled out on his seat, his legs stretched wide apart, his thumbs in the armholes of his waistcoat, his head flung back, and his eyes tight closed in an ecstasy of pleasure as his heart warmed to the commonplaces of the vulgar tune.

Louder and shriller he sang until the music of the accordion and the sturdy bellowings of two passengers at the rear of the 'bus made no more impression than the murmur of bees. At last it ended in a delirious scream from the negroid young man, who held an awful top note till the veins in his neck swelled and the colour of his face turned to an apoplectic purple. Then like a punctured balloon he collapsed, and rattling windows and rumbling machinery were heard once more sweet as summer rain.

" We'll hae nae mair o' that."

The speaker was a mild little man with a shrivelled face and pathetic monkey eyes. But for all his seeming meekness his voice recorded stern disapproval of the negroid young man and his dreadful song.

"Johnnie," he said, "Johnnie, will ye sing ma favourite, ' The Bonnie Lass o' Ballochmyle ' ? "

But Johnnie paid no heed. He was absorbed in the happy rhythm of quadrilles; and, balancing himself in the narrow space between two seats, pantomimed the "paddy bash and bow to partners." His elbows were squeezed into his sides and his leg of mutton hands thrust out from his hips. He threw back his head, stuck out his chest, assumed the half-anxious, half-vacuous smile of the earnest dancer, and seemed to flow across the floor of the 'bus to meet his partner, and then to retreat again with his head and shoulders now drooping. Two waggles of his hips, an upward thrust of his hands, a triumphant "hooch!" and the pantomime ended suddenly as the lurching 'bus threw him off his balance and tumbled him in a heap on his seat.

The mild little man called out again for "The Bonnie Lass," but Johnnie shook his head dourly.

"Aw, Johnnie, please, ma favourite." The little man was so plaintive and insistent that it seemed another refusal must make him burst into dismal weeping. Johnnie yielded with little grace, and as Charlie and the accordion conducted some preliminary investigations into the vagaries of the tune, the negroid young man spat with venomous contempt. But the little man was justified in his importunity, for Johnnie, middle-aged and moon-faced with a large and wanton mouth, sang with the tenderness and sweetness of a young lover, and benign contentment oozed from the little man. The song carried us through the mean and crowded streets until it ended as the 'bus lurched heavily round the corner by Duke Street prison.

"We're hame," said Charlie, who had not spoken a word since I joined the 'bus forty minutes earlier, and as he began to pack his accordion into its case we all grew self-conscious, a little uneasy at our cheerful abandon. The atmosphere reeked of cigarette smoke, fish and chips, and warm bodies, and I longed for the refreshment of a hot bath. As we stepped from the 'bus the rain fell cold and dismal.

א